The *Best* of the
Appalachian Trail
Day Hikes

Also by Victoria and Frank Logue
The Best of The Appalachian Trail: Overnight Hikes
The Appalachian Trail Backpacker
Appalachian Trail Fun Book

Also by Victoria Logue
Backpacking in the 90s: Tips, Techniques and Secrets
Camping in the 90s: Tips, Techniques and Secrets

The *Best* of the Appalachian Trail

Day Hikes

Victoria and Frank Logue

Menasha Ridge Press
Birmingham, Alabama

Appalachian Trail Conference
Harpers Ferry, West Virginia

Please Note:

The hikes in this book describe the route of the Appalachian Trail at the time of publication. But, the trail is occasionally relocated and the route may differ at the time of your hike. Severe damage to the trail caused by storms may impact on your hike as well. If the white blazes differ from the hike described in this book, follow the trail as it is marked.

Neither the authors, nor the publishers, can warrant your safety while on the hikes in this book. Use caution and your best judgement. If you have any changes or suggestions, the authors may be contacted in care of the publishers at either address given below.

© 1994 by Victoria and Frank Logue

All rights reserved
Printed in the United States of America
Published by Menasha Ridge Press and The Appalachian Trail Conference
First Edition, Third Printing

Cover photo of fall foliage taken on the A.T./Long Trail
near Little Rock Pond, Vermont by Frank Logue

Drawings by Dian McCray

Woodcuts by Leslie Cummins

Library of Congress Cataloging-in-Publication Data

Logue, Victoria, 1961-
    The best of the Appalachian Trail: day hikes / Victoria and Frank Logue. — 1st ed.
        p. cm.
    ISBN 0-89732-138-3
    1. Hiking—Appalachian Trail—Guidebooks. 2. Appalachian Trail—
Guidebooks. I. Logue, Frank, 1963- . II. Title.
GV199.42.A68L646 1994
796.5'.'0974—dc20   94-37977
                                                CIP

Menasha Ridge Press
3169 Cahaba Heights Road
Birmingham, Alabama 35243

Appalachian Trail Conference
Post Office Box 807
Harpers Ferry, West Virginia 25425
(304) 535-6311

For Willie Frank Logue
the best grandmother a boy could have.
—Frank

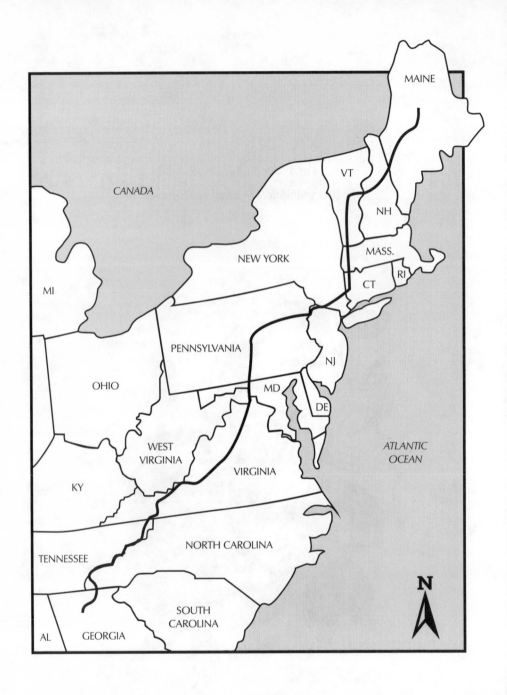

CONTENTS

INTRODUCTION

Red leaves rustle in the wind and break loose from their branches. The soft sound made by thousands of leaves as they fall onto the already littered forest floor can barely be heard over the burbling, pattering, and splashing sounds from Little Black Branch. The small creek runs alongside the Appalachian Trail on a hike from USFS 10 to Little Rock Pond. We walk over to the stream to show our then two-year-old daughter, Griffin, the water she could hear splashing just off the trail. In a wide, shallow pool, red maple leaves circle around and around, caught in an eddy. The wet leaves seem irridescent, lit by the sunlight streaming through the trees on this crisp October morning.

That short, easy hike was the perfect way to spend the morning. There was plenty of time for Griffin to get down and walk on her own, and the pond surrounded by Vermont's peak foliage was a tremendous sight. This book was written to introduce you to just that kind of experience—the best day hikes on the 2,100-mile Appalachian Trail.

History of the Appalachian Trail

The idea for a trail running the length of the Appalachian Mountains was first considered in the early part of this century. The Appalachian Trail, as we know it, was the vision of Benton MacKaye (rhymes with sky) and others who had been thinking about the concept for more than ten years. In 1921, MacKaye took the initiative and launched the project through an article in *The Journal of the American Institute of Architects*.

In that first article, MacKaye wrote about the purpose of the trail:

"There would be a chance to catch a breath, to study the dynamic forces of nature and the possibilities of shifting to them the burdens now carried on the backs of men ... Industry would come to be seen in its true perspective—as a means in life and not as an end in itself."

MacKaye's original intent was to construct a trail from "the highest peak in the North to the highest peak in the South—from Mount Washington (New Hampshire) to Mt. Mitchell (North Carolina)." He envisioned a fourfold plan including the trail, shelters, community camps, and food and farm camps. The camps never came about. And although MacKaye's larger economic plan for the Appalachian Trail never gained support, his main purpose—an opportunity for American families to commune with nature—is the reason for the trail's continuing existence today.

Within a year after MacKaye's article appeared in the architectural journal, the New York-New Jersey Trail Conference began work on a new trail with the goal of making it part of the Appalachian Trail. In the Hudson River Valley, the new Bear Mountain Bridge would connect the future section in New England with Harriman State Park and eventually with Delaware Water Gap in Pennsylvania.

In 1925, MacKaye and others formed the Appalachian Trail Conference (ATC) to guide the project to completion. By 1936, Myron H. Avery, who would be president of the Appalachian Trail Conference for twenty years, had finished measuring the flagged route of the Appalachian Trail. He became the first 2,000-miler a year before the completion of the trail.

On August 14, 1937, the Civilian Conservation Corps (CCC) workers cleared the final link in the 2,025-mile Appalachian Trail. On a high ridge connecting Spaulding and Sugarloaf Mountains in Maine, a six-person CCC crew cut the last two miles of trail. The finished route of the Appalachian Trail was not as originally envisioned by MacKaye; the final product was longer, stretching from Mt. Oglethorpe (the southern terminus of the eastern Blue Ridge) in Georgia to Mt. Katahdin in Maine's Baxter State Park.

The trail did not remain complete for long. The next year, a hurricane demolished miles of trail in the northeast, while the decision to connect the Skyline Drive (under construction at the time) with the Blue Ridge Parkway displaced another 120 miles of trail in Virginia. The trail was not made continuous again until 1951, after the world had settled down from World War II.

In 1968, President Lyndon Johnson signed the National Trails System Act and made the Appalachian Trail the first National Scenic Trail. The act charged federal agencies with the task of buying lands to protect the trailway from encroaching development, but ten years passed before the government acted and began protecting the trail lands. By 1993, less than two percent of the A.T. remained unprotected.

Perhaps the most amazing aspect of the world's largest greenway is that the trail was conceived and developed by private citizens. As a testament to the work carried out for decades by volunteers, the federal government left the management of the trail to a private non-profit group—the Appalachian Trail Conference—even after the footpath was brought under federal protection.

Selecting a Hike

When we set out to pick the best of the A.T., we decided that although the hikes could use side trails, they would have to mostly be on the A.T. to qualify for the book. But there are a few hikes in this book that bend that rule. These few hikes were so spectacular that although they use little of the Appalachian Trail, they just couldn't be left out.

The hike descriptions often suggest more than great hikes. The information provided will also tell you good times to hike in the area or when to avoid hiking there. Interesting flora and fauna is mentioned as is notable history. To help you pick out a hike that offers just what you are looking for, several easy-to-find pieces of information are located at the top of each hike description: the hike rating, length and time of the hike, and icons denoting major attractions along the way.

Icons

Each hike has one or more icons that show the major attractions along the way. The icons (mountain peak, scenic view, pond or lake, waterfall or stream, river, historic area, or bird-watching area) are intended to give you an easy-to-identify symbol that you can use when you flip through the book looking for a hike.

| Mountain Peak | Scenic View | Pond or River | Waterfall | Historic Area | Bird-Watching |

Ratings
The hikes are rated as easy, moderate, or strenuous. Easy denotes hikes with little elevation gain or loss that are not more than ten miles in length. Moderate hikes have no long, steep climbs or descents but there may be some short, steep grades or long, gradual ascents. Strenuous hikes are steep, and sometimes long, and should not be attempted by inexperienced hikers or people in poor physical condition.

Length and Hike Times
A good way to gauge hiking time on the trail is to allow a half hour for each mile to be hiked as well as an additional hour for each thousand-feet of elevation gained. This pace allows for a leisurely hike with some time to stop at overlooks and other points of interest. The hikes in this book can certainly be done faster or slower, but this formula will give you an idea of how long you will need to walk.

Equipment for Day Hikes
One of the benefits of day hiking (as opposed to backpacking) is that you are relatively unburdened by equipment. There are a few things, however, that every well-prepared day hiker should have, as well as a few optional items that you might want to take along to make your trip more enjoyable.

You need to be dressed in comfortable clothes that don't constrict your movement too much. For many hikes in this book, a sturdy pair of shorts, a t-shirt, and good walking shoes or hiking boots will be adequate. You will also need a daypack or fanny pack to carry what little gear you need. For all but the shortest of hikes (a mile or less), you should carry water in a one-liter (minimum) canteen, and raingear, such as a rainsuit, poncho or umbrella.

Items you may want to consider carrying in your pack include a small first aid kit, a lighter or matches, toilet paper and a trowel, and a map or guidebook. We also suggest that you carry only a photocopy of the pages you need from this book rather than the entire book when you hike.

If you are going to be hiking at high altitudes or above treeline, carry some warm clothing because the temperature on the mountaintops can be much lower than in the valley. Other items you may want to carry in your pack include a camera and film, binoculars, and wildlife guides.

Boots
Hiking boots range in price from $50 to $250 and are generally divided into

three categories: heavyweight, mediumweight and lightweight. Heavyweight boots, which weigh more than 4 pounds, are generally designed for technically demanding climbs on ice (usually with crampons) or on snow or alpine rock. You will not need heavyweights for the hikes in this book unless you choose to climb Katahdin in the dead of winter.

Mediumweight boots, which weigh from 2.5 to 4 pounds, are almost entirely made of leather, though many blend in a combination of tough fabric as well. Mediumweights are ideal for the broadest range of hiking situations.

Lightweight boots, which weigh less than 2.5 pounds, are almost always made with a combination of leather and a "breathable" fabric. Lightweights rarely require a "breaking-in" period and are tough enough to handle any of the hikes in this book.

When purchasing a boot, the important factor to keep in mind is proper fit. Even the best boots will make you miserable if they are not fitted properly. This is best done in a store, but you can also purchase boots by mail order if the company has a good return policy. Once you buy the boots, make sure to break them in well around town before heading out into the woods. If lightweights fit properly, they won't require a breaking in, but even these boots can be purchased too small or too big, too narrow or too wide. Be prepared with moleskin to treat "hot spots"before blisters develop.

Daypacks

Because most daypacks are made in the same teardrop style, the important thing to look at is how well the pack is made. Inexpensive daypacks can be purchased at any discount store, but if they are poorly padded and have little support, you won't have hiked a mile before you regret the purchase.

Leather-bottomed packs are the most durable and carry the load better because they support the weight rather than collapse beneath it. Make sure the shoulder straps on your daypack are secure. This is the first place that daypacks fall apart because you carry the weight on your shoulders as opposed to your hips. To prevent ripping, a number of daypacks have extra reinforcement where the shoulder straps connect to the sack.

Another feature to look for is padding at the back of the pack. The more reinforced this section, the less likely you'll be poked and prodded by the objects inside the pack.

Other features to look for in daypacks include convenient loading through a top or front panel, pockets for smaller items (some daypacks feature a special loop to hold keys), a waist strap to keep the back from bouncing against your back, padded shoulder straps, and lash points for extra gear. Daypacks are usually less than $100 and most manufacturers feature a variety to choose from.

Fanny Packs

Fanny packs can be used on day hikes in place of a daypack, but they are not as comfortable as daypacks; they do not distribute the weight as well and usually cannot carry as much as you might like to bring. They can be used along with a daypack or alone (if you have a partner carrying a daypack).

Some hikers use fanny packs worn in reverse, snug across their bellies with the strap fastened in the small of the back. Cameras, water, snacks, data books, maps, guides or whatever you need can be quickly accessed using this method.

When purchasing a fanny pack, make sure the belt is well-padded for comfort, and the sack is sturdy enough to carry the load you intend for it. Some fanny packs are designed to carry only very light loads and will sag if heavy objects are placed in them. Also, if the fabric is thin, you may get poked and prodded by the objects inside.

Equipment Checklist
❑ Hiking boots
❑ Daypack and/or fanny pack
❑ Pocket knife*
❑ Food and beverage for length of hike
❑ Raingear
❑ Sweater or coat †
❑ Bandanas*
❑ Toilet paper and trowel*
❑ Maps and guidebooks*
❑ Sunglasses*
❑ First aid kit (including moleskin and space blanket)*
❑ Camera and film*
❑ Insect repellent and sunscreen or lotion†
❑ Hiking stick*

*optional equipment
†seasonal equipment

Minimum Impact

Minimum impact camping is a philosophy once summed up by the National Park Service as, "Take nothing but pictures, leave nothing but footprints." The following sub-headings discuss measures you can take to help eliminate traces of your presence along the trail. This is not a list of rules but rather a way of living that is becoming increasingly important to adopt. If these techniques are not used by everyone (and currently they're not), the A.T. will lose its natural beauty. Nature is resilient, but its ability to fight back is limited. A little bit of help goes a long way toward improving the world we're escaping to. If everyone pitches in, we'll be able to enjoy our backcountry experiences even more.

Carry Out All of Your Trash

Pack it in, pack it out, and you're already one giant step toward improving the environment you've escaped to. Keep a sack handy to store your trash in. Trash includes everything, even organic material. Orange peels, apple cores and egg shells may strike you as natural trash, easily biodegradable. Why not toss it into the brush? Because it takes five months for an orange peel to rot and become one with the earth.

There is nothing worse than heading back into the woods to relieve yourself and discovering a trail of paper proving you weren't the first to have this idea at this spot. Soggy, used toilet paper is probably one of the uglier reminders of human presence.

Following trails littered with cigarette butts is disheartening. If you want to smoke, that's your prerogative, but don't think of the outdoors as one big ashtray. Not only is the litter of cigarette butts ugly, but it only takes one stray spark to start a forest fire that will turn the woods into a huge ashtray.

Carry Out Trash Left by Others

The trails abound with trash. For some reason, people who wouldn't dare throw trash on the ground at home do so freely in the outdoors. Unfortunately, the enviro-conscious do not outnumber the users and abusers of America's trails. We have to make up for their ignorance and sloth by picking up after them.

You can make the outdoors an even better place by stopping occasionally to pick up other people's trash. You don't have to be ridiculous and carry out nasty toilet paper or rotting organic material, but you can take a minute to cover it with leaves, moss, dirt, and twigs. Pick up trash, you'll find you feel a lot better about yourself.

Switchbacks
Stay on designated trails; switchbacks are there for a reason. They slow down the trail erosion on steep climbs. It may seem easier to scramble up the hillside to the next section of trail, but if too many people did that, rain would start using the newly exposed earth as a watercourse, washing away both trail and mountain in its wake. You may curse the person who blazed it and those who attempt to keep it passable for you, but remember that just about any trail you hike was built and maintained by volunteers.

Solid Waste Management
In other words, how to dispose of your excrement. Disposing of your feces when backpacking is absolutely necessary. Always, always, always (I can't say it too many times) dig a hole. More importantly, make sure you're at least 150 feet from the nearest water source. If you're hiking alongside a stream, climb up. There's more to being green than just packing out your trash. Disposing properly of your solid waste will keep the wilderness much more appealing.

Trail Maintenance
Give back to the trail and the hiking community by becoming involved in trail maintenance. Maintaining a section of existing trail or helping out with blazing new trails is a good way to payback the outdoors for the good times you have received from it. Trails are beginning to criss-cross the entire country, and there is sure to be a new or old trail somewhere near you. Contact your local trail clubs to see what you can do to help out. Most backpacking shops can tell you about clubs in your area.

The entire Appalachian Trail is maintained by volunteers. To find out more about the clubs that maintain the Appalachian Trail, contact the Appalachian Trail Conference (see appendix).

Finding Solitude
Many hikers retreat to the Appalachian Trail seeking a wilderness experience, only to find themselves on a crowded section of trail sharing their "wilderness experience" with more hikers than they bargained for. Here are a few tips for finding a little solitude on America's most popular long distance trail.

Start your hike early in the morning. We once took this advice to the extreme and enjoyed the best hike of our lives for the effort. We started climbing Katahdin at 2:30 A.M. and arrived at Baxter Peak by 5:30 A.M., in time for the sunrise. The view was spectacular and we didn't share the summit with another hiker. That was on a Labor Day weekend, when later in the day hikers marched in a long, single-file line from Baxter Peak to Pamola Peak. By making an extra effort to get up early (and hike the tricky section of trail in the dark), we had the peak to ourselves on perhaps the busiest day of the year.

Another way to find your own piece of the Appalachian Trail is to hike during the off-season. Roan Highlands on the Tennessee/North Carolina state line is very crowded during peak bloom of the rhododendron garden. In June, visitors flock to see the awesome spectacle—thousands of big catawba rhododendrons in bloom at once—but during the winter we have camped alone on the summit. We didn't see the rhododendron in bloom, but the snow-covered mountain was a magnificent sight.

A third way to find solitude on the country's most popular long distance trail is to discover your own special places. After enjoying the hikes in this book, branch out and discover more of the trail on your own. To help you in your search, the Appalachian Trail Conference publishes a set of eleven guidebooks. They cover the entire 2,100-mile footpath, mile by mile.

Safety

Trouble is rare on the Appalachian Trail, but theft is not uncommon. Cars parked at trailheads are usually targeted for break-ins because theives know that the owner will be away for awhile. Do not leave visible anything worth stealing, or better yet, leave all valuables at home. Also, do not leave any notes on your car stating where you are going and how long you intend to be gone. You might as well advertise for your car to be broken into.

It is doubtful you will run into any troublesome humans on the A.T., but if you do run into someone that gives you a bad feeling, keep moving.

Weather is something else you need to be concerned about when hiking. While it is neither impossible nor necessarily uncomfortable to hike in rain or snow or intense heat, there are certain precautions you should take. Clothing suitable to the situation is important—raingear for rain, layered clothing for snow and cold weather, and lightweight, porous clothing for hot days. With the appropriate clothing, you can go a long ways toward avoiding both hypothermia and hyperthermia.

Some of the hikes mentioned in this book are along sections of trail that are above treeline or in other exposed areas. In some cases, an alternate bad weather route is available, but in many places, this is not an option. If inclement weather is predicted, it might be wise to take a rain check. For above treeline hikes, carry along raingear just in case because storms can form suddenly at high elevations.

Getting lost is rarely a problem on the A.T., but anyone can become distracted and miss a blaze that indicates a turn. The Appalachian Trail is marked with white blazes at least every quarter mile, and usually more often. Most maintainers try to blaze so you can see the next blaze as soon as you have passed the previous one. So, if you have walked for more than five minutes without seeing a blaze, it would be wise to backtrack until you see a blaze and then continue on your way.

First Aid
The risk of serious injury on a day hike is not high, but being unprepared would be tempting fate. You can still get stung by a bee, twist an ankle, develop blisters, become hypothermic or have a heat stroke. The following information will give you some ideas about how to deal with these situations if they arise.

Hypothermia
Shivering, numbness, drowsiness and marked muscular weakness are the first signs of hypothermia. These symptoms are followed by mental confusion, impairment of judgement, slurred speech, failing eyesight and unconsciousness. The most serious warning sign of hypothermia occurs when the shivering stops. If the victim stops shivering, he is close to death.

Fortunately, hypothermia is easy to treat. If you or a friend is feeling hypothermic, get warm. In the case of a day hike, this may mean nothing more than hurrying back to your car, stripping yourself of wet clothes, and turning the heater on. If you are hiking with friends, they may be able to help you get warm. As long as you are hiking, your body will continue to try and warm itself. Keeping still could mean death, unless you are taking action to warm back up.

Hyperthermia
This ailment develops in three steps: heat cramps, heat exhaustion and heat stroke. The best treatment for hyperthermia is prevention. If you are hiking in particularly hot weather, make sure you maintain a continual and

consistent intake of fluids. Dehydration is what usually leads to heat-related ailments. Also, if hiking is making you too hot, take a break, find some shade, drink some water, and give your body a few minutes to cool off.

If you progress to heat cramps (legs or abdomen begin to cramp), you are on your way to heat exhaustion and heat stroke. Take a break and sip water slowly. It is best to add a bit of salt to the water if possible. Rather than continue hiking, you should call it a day, and if possible, return to your car.

Heat exhaustion can follow heat cramps. Although the body temperature remains fairly normal, the skin is pale, cool and clammy; you may also feel faint, weak, nauseated and dizzy. Sit in the shade and sip water. Lower your head between your knees to relieve the dizziness. You can also lie down, loosen your clothes (or take them off if you're not shy), and elevate your feet about one foot. Bathe in cool water if there is any available. Vomiting signals a serious condition and medical help should be sought.

When suffering from heat stroke, the skin becomes hot, red and dry; the pulse, rapid and strong. Unconsciousness is common. The victim should be undressed and bathed in cool water until the skin temperature is lowered, but do not over chill the victim, which can be as dangerous as overheating. Medical attention should be sought as soon as possible.

Blisters
Blisters develop slowly and can make you miserable. As soon as you feel a hot spot, cover it with moleskin. If not treated properly, blisters can become infected. If you do get a blister, leave it unbroken; if it is already broken, treat it like an open wound, cleansing it and bandaging it. Do not continue to hike if you are in too much pain.

Lightning
Lightning kills more people each year than any other natural disaster, including earthquakes, floods and tornadoes. If you get caught on the trail during a lightning storm, there are a few things you can do to reduce your chances of being struck. Avoid bodies of water and low places where water can collect. Avoid high places, ridges, open places, tall objects, metal objects, rock outcroppings, wet caves and ditches. If possible, find a stand of trees and sit with your knees pulled up to your chest, head bowed and arms hugging knees.

Bee Stings

Although most insects (other than black flies, deer flies, and ticks) will try to avoid you, bees (yellow jackets in particular) are attracted to food, beverages, perfume, scented soaps and lotions, deodorant, and bright-colored (and dark) clothing. Yellow jackets nest anywhere that provides cover—logs, trees, even underground. And they don't mind stinging more than once!

If you're sensitive to stings, carry an oral antihistamine to reduce swelling. A topical antihistamine, such as Benadryl, will help reduce itching. If you are allergic and a potential victim of anaphylactic shock, carry an Anakit whenever you hike. The Anakit, which must be prescribed by a doctor, contains a couple of injections of epinephrine as well as antihistamine tablets. If you use the kit, seek medical attention as soon as possible.

Other Pests

Deer, bear, boar, moose, raccoons, snakes, skunk and porcupines can all be found along the A.T., but these animals rarely cause problems for hikers; particularly day hikers.

Bee stings, as discussed above, present an immediate and potentially fatal problem, but there are other insects on the trail to watch out for—no-see-ums, black flies, deer flies, horse flies, mosquitos and ticks. The first five insects all produce itchy, painful bites that can be treated with a topical or oral antihistamine (or both, depending on how badly you react to their bites). Wearing lots of clothing, including a hat, will put the bugs at a disadvantage, but you may be uncomfortable. A bug repellent that is a thirty-five percent DEET works best.

Along the A.T., the tick is the biggest problem because some are infected with Lyme disease. You will need to take a little extra precaution. The tiny (about the size of a pinhead) deer tick is the carrier of Lyme disease. Whenever you hike in tick country (tall grass and underbrush), make sure you check yourself afterwards for ticks. It takes a while for a tick to become imbedded, so a thorough check at the end of the day will help you catch the tick before it catches you.

Wear a hat, long sleeve shirt, and pants with cuffs tucked into socks to discourage ticks. Too uncomfortable? Use a repellent with permethrin and stick to the center of the trail to avoid brushing against branches and shrubs. Ticks, like mosquitos, are attracted to heat and have been known to hang around for months waiting for a hot body to pass by. Try wearing light colored clothing so you'll be able to see the ticks more clearly.

If a tick attaches itself to your body, the best way to remove it is by grasping the skin directly below where the tick is attached and removing the tick along with a small piece of skin. Then carefully wash the bite with soap and water. Following its removal, keep an eye out for the symptoms of Lyme disease: fever, headache, and pain and stiffness in joints and muscles. If left untreated, Lyme disease can produce lifelong impairment of muscular and nervous systems, chronic arthritis, brain injury, and in ten percent of victims, crippling arthritis. If you suspect Lyme, see your doctor. Tick season is from April to October with a peak from May to July.

Hantavirus

This deadly disease made the news in 1994 with an outbreak in the Four Corners area of the southwest. About that time, the Trail community learned that an A.T. thru-hiker had contracted hantavirus about 18 months earlier while hiking through southwest Virginia. The hiker had been hospitalized for a month in 1992 with the disease, but returned to the A.T. in 1994 to complete his thru-hike. Meanwhile, many hikers were left with grave concerns about this new infectious disease.

Hantavirus is rare and difficult to contract. You must have contact with the feces or urine of deer mice, or breathe air infected with the disease through evaporated droppings. Federal and state authorities have trapped and tested mice in shelters in southwest Virginia without finding evidence of the disease. To be safe, avoid all contact with mice and their droppings. Air out a closed, mice-infested structure an hour before occupying it.

Dogs

If you hike with a dog, you may have additional problems. Dogs can be sprayed by skunks, barbed by porcupines, and bitten by snakes. Plus, if you choose to hike with a dog, be prepared for your friend to scare up trouble. Dogs like to find dead things and roll in them, competing with the skunk for the most obnoxious odor.

Dogs can also cause other problems. A.T. hikers have been bitten by other hikers' dogs. If your dog does not like other people, leave him at home or keep him restrained while hiking. If you come upon a threatening dog, a hiking stick makes a good weapon. (*NOTE:* Dogs need as much water as you do on hot days.)

MAINE

MAINE

The Appalachian Trail in Maine is more rugged and remote than in any of the other thirteen trail states. The northern terminus of the A.T. is at Baxter Peak on top of Katahdin in Maine's Baxter State Park. From that peak, you can look to the southwest and see the Maine lake country that the A.T. crosses in this part of the state.

The trail in Maine traverses several prominent mountains including the twin peaks of the Bigelow Range, the Crockers, Saddleback, Old Blue, the Baldpates and the Mahoosuc Range. In the Mahoosucs, the A.T. features what is often described as the "toughest mile." This section through Mahoosuc Notch is a testament to trail builders' imagination and a hiker's stamina; here the A.T. goes over and under an incredible boulder-filled notch. The A.T. continues over Goose Eye and Mount Carlo on its way to the state line with New Hampshire.

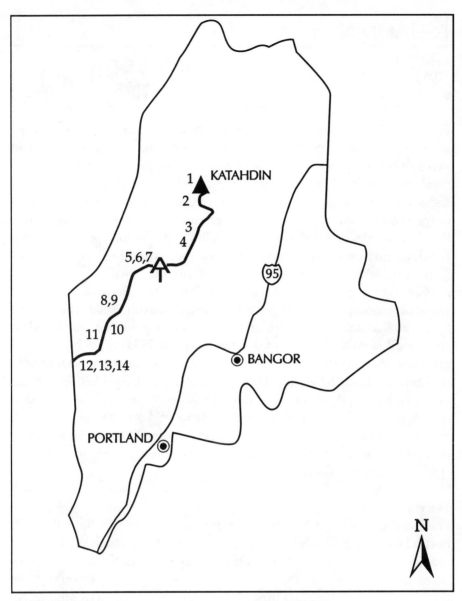

1. Katahdin
2. Baxter Ponds Loop
3. Gulf Hagas
4. Chairback Mountain
5. Avery & West Peaks of Bigelow
6. West Peak and the Horns
7. Horns Pond
8. Piazza Rock
9. Saddleback Mountain
10. Dunn Notch and Falls
11. Baldpate Mountain
12. The Eyebrow
13. Old Speck
14. Speck Pond

KATAHDIN

STRENUOUS
10.4 miles roundtrip
9 1/2 hours

From Katahdin's Baxter Peak, the surrounding lakes shimmer in the sunlight thousands of feet below. Katahdin affords one of the most expansive wilderness views east of the Mississippi River and one of the most outstanding hikes on the A.T. Katahdin, known by the Abenaki Indians as "Kette-Adene," meaning greatest mountain, is not part of a range of mountains. Instead, the gray granite monolith towers alone over the Central Maine forests. The A.T. follows the Hunt Spur Trail from Katahdin Stream Campground along the route used in 1804 by Charles Turner, Jr., who made the first known ascent of the peak.

Katahdin is the crown jewel of Baxter State Park. The idea for the park was championed by Maine's Governor, Percival Baxter. But during his five terms in the state legislature and one term as governor, he failed to convince his colleagues to create the park. In 1931, after his term as governor ended, he bought more than 6,500 acres on and around Katahdin and gave the land to the state. By the time of his death in 1969, Baxter had extended his initial grant to more than 201,000 acres and created the largest park east of the Mississippi devoted solely to wilderness use. As a condition of the grant, Baxter maintained that the area "forever be left in its natural wild state." In Baxter State Park, recreational use is secondary to wilderness preservation.

The Hike
From the trailhead at Katahdin Stream Campground, follow the A.T. north. Hike along Katahdin Stream for 1.2 miles and reach the fifty-foot cascade, Katahdin Stream Falls. After passing the falls, the trail continues its moderate ascent for another 1.6 miles before passing through "The Boulders." The Boulders are tricky to traverse, even in good weather. Steel bars driven into the rock offer hand and foot holds to help you climb up and over the jumble of rocks and begin the steady, steep ascent of Hunt Spur.

Just over 3.5 miles from Katahdin Stream Campground is "The Gateway," the rim of the tableland. It is a large, relatively flat boulder field left by the glacier that planed off the top of the mountain. Reach Thoreau

Spring, named for the famous philosopher whose attempted ascent of Katahdin ended here, in .5 mile. The spring does not offer a reliable source of water in dry weather. From Thoreau Spring, 1 mile of easy to moderate climbs along the boulder field leads you to Baxter Peak, the northern terminus of the A.T.

The return trip will go faster, but allow yourself plenty of time to get off the mountain. Katahdin is a difficult day hike, but the walk is well worth the effort. Be sure to leave early and carry plenty of warm clothes and rain gear no matter what weather is expected below.

Despite the difficulty, this hike is extremely popular. One year, we climbed the mountain on Labor Day weekend with what seemed like a continuous line of hikers all along the route. Like all backcountry areas, the mountain is less crowded during the week. For more information, contact Reservation Clerk, Baxter State Park, 64 Balsam Drive, Millinocket, Maine 04462, or phone (207) 723-5140.

Trailhead Directions

Katahdin Stream Campground is located along the Perimeter Road in Baxter State Park about 8 miles from the Togue Pond Gate. The gate is located about 20 miles from Millinocket, Maine on Baxter Park Road.

BAXTER PONDS LOOP

EASY
3.5 mile loop
2 hours

This loop is an easy leg-stretcher in Maine's Baxter State Park using both the A.T. and the Grassy Pond Trail. You will pass four small ponds, where moose and other wildlife can often be seen. In good weather, you will be afforded excellent views of Mount Katahdin and other lesser peaks in the area. If you are planning on visiting Baxter Park with children, the Ponds Loop is your best bet for an enjoyable afternoon.

Katahdin is the crown jewel of Baxter State Park. The idea for the park was championed by Maine's Governor, Percival Baxter. But during his five terms in the state legislature and one term as governor, he failed to convince his colleagues to create the park. In 1931, after his term as governor ended, he bought more than 6,500 acres on and around Katahdin and gave the land to the state. By the time of his death in 1969, Baxter had extended his initial grant to more than 201,000 acres and created the largest park east of the Mississippi devoted solely to wilderness use. As a condition of the grant, Baxter maintained that the area "forever be left in its natural wild state." In Baxter State Park, recreational use is secondary to wilderness preservation.

The Hike

From Daicey Pond Campground, follow the A.T. north for .5 mile. You will be skirting the north shore of Daicey Pond. In another .5 mile, the A.T. turns sharply left. Continue to follow the shore of Daicey Pond along the Grassy Pond Trail, which is marked by blue blazes.

In .25 mile, the trail turns away from the shore of the pond to follow along an old tote road. Three-quarters of a mile after turning on the tote road, a side trail leads .1 mile to the south end of Grassy Pond. Pass the outlet of Grassy Pond and continue through a swamp on bog bridges.

At mile 2, reach the park's perimeter road, which is about .1 mile from Katahdin Stream Campground. Turn left and follow the A.T. for another .5 mile, heading away from the perimeter road. Here, the trail skirts Tracy Pond with fine views of OJI and Doubletop Mountains. In another .1 mile, you will skirt the shore of Elbow Pond and cross its outlet.

From the outlet, hike another .5 mile to the junction with the Grassy Pond Trail. Follow the white blazes around the north shore of the pond and return to Daicey Pond Campground.

Trailhead Directions

Daicey Pond Campground is located about 1 mile off the perimeter road in Baxter State Park, which is about 11 miles from the Togue Pond Gate. The gate is located about 20 miles from Millinocket, Maine, on Baxter Park Road.

GULF HAGAS

MODERATE
8.6 miles roundtrip
4 1/2 hours

The Gulf Hagas day hike is the first to bend the rule about using the A.T. Of the 8.6 miles of this hike, only 3.4 are on the A.T. The Gulf's deep slate canyon made it easy to bend the rule. It is a wilderness area of astounding beauty and can only be reached via the A.T.

Gulf Hagas Brook cuts its way through the canyon in a series of spectacular waterfalls. The pools below the falls create number of swimming holes that hearty hikers may want to take advantage of. You'll want to take care though; several of the descents from the trail to the brook are quite steep and rocky. The easiest falls to reach for swimming are at the top and bottom of the Gulf Hagas Loop. This loop makes an especially good fall foliage hike if you're not interested in swimming.

The Hike
From the parking lot on the St. Regis Logging Road, take the A.T. north. In about .1 mile, reach the ford of the West Branch of the Pleasant River. The cold river water is usually only knee deep, which makes for a relatively easy crossing. The rocks can be slippery, though, and you will need to go slow and be sure of your footing to avoid getting wet.

One mile beyond the river ford puts you in the center of The Hermitage, a stand of one hundred foot white pines owned by the Maine Chapter of the Nature Conservancy. This type of tree was once used for the masts of sailing ships.

Just 1.7 miles from the road parking lot, reach the junction with the Gulf Hagas Trail. The Gulf Hagas Trail is a loop hike of 5.2 miles that begins and ends at this junction. You can cut your hike short by hiking out and back on a portion of the Gulf Hagas Trail instead of completing the loop described here.

Hike .5 mile to a side trail leading .1 mile to a worthwhile view of the canyon at Hammond Street Pitch. Here, the Gulf is more than ninety feet deep. Just over .25 mile further, the trail turns right and another side trail leads to a view of the canyon.

Hike another 1 mile to a short side trail leading to the base of Buttermilk

Falls, and another .5 mile to Stair Falls. The trail reaches the head of The Gulf in .75 mile and turns sharply right, leaving the river behind.

In .25 mile, reach the Pleasant River Road. Descend back to the starting point of the loop at its junction with the A.T. and then return to the St. Regis Logging Road via the A.T.

Trailhead Directions
From Brownville Junction, Maine, take Maine 11 for 5.5 miles to Katahdin Iron Works Road. From Maine 11, it is 7 miles to the Katahdin Iron Works Gate. (There might be a fee.) After passing through the gate, take your first right and your next left onto the St. Regis Logging road. The A.T. crosses the St. Regis Logging Road about 6 miles from the Katahdin Iron Works Gate.

CHAIRBACK MOUNTAIN

STRENUOUS
6.4 miles roundtrip
5 hours

This rugged, rocky climb affords spectacular views of the Pleasant River Valley and the entire White Cap Range. The features of this hike include open peaks, cliffs, mountain tarns and beautiful spruce-fir forests. Less than 2 miles into the hike, a side trail leads .25 mile downhill to the north shore of East Chairback Pond, one of three mountain tarns in the Barren-Chairback Range. Chairback Mountain lies at the eastern end of the Barren-Chairback Range which extends 10 miles to the west. On especially clear days, Mount Katahdin can be seen to the northeast.

The Hike
From the parking lot on the St. Regis Logging Road, follow the A.T. south. The trail follows the road for a short distance, turns left, and ascends steeply out of the valley. (The road continues another 2.3 miles to the Chairback Mountain Camps on Long Pond.) In nearly .5 mile, begin to ascend more gradually, passing through thick conifer growth along a ridge. At mile 1.3, you will reach the high point of the ridge. Here, a side trail descends .25 mile to the north shore of East Chairback Pond.

Continue along the A.T., and cross three low ridges to the east of the pond as you ascend Chairback Mountain. At mile 2.1, reach the base of the main ascent of Chairback. Hike just over .5 mile to where the trail crosses partially open ledges below Chairback Mountain's prominent cliffs and ascend very steeply around the cliffs. Reach the summit of Chairback Mountain (elevation 2,219 feet) at mile 3.2.

Return to the parking area by retracing your footsteps north on the A.T.

Trailhead Directions
From Brownville Junction, Maine, take Maine 11 for 5.5 miles to Katahdin Ironworks Road. From Maine 11, it is 7 miles to the Katahdin Iron Works Gate (there might be a fee). After passing through the gate, take your first right, and then your next left onto the St. Regis Logging Road. The A.T. crosses the St. Regis Logging Road about 6 miles from the Katahdin Iron Works Gate.

AVERY AND WEST PEAKS OF BIGELOW

STRENUOUS
8.2 miles roundtrip
7 1/2 hours

This hike uses very little of the A.T., but it must be another exception to the rule. The Bigelow Range is probably the most outstanding in Maine. Bigelow is known as "Maine's Second Mountain" next to Katahdin. This long, east-west range consists of six major peaks as well as a number of minor ones. The most spectacular of these are Avery (East) and West Peaks, which are followed closely by the Horns. This hike also uses the Firewardens Trail. Although this trail provides the shortest route to Avery and West Peak, it is also the steepest ascent and descent.

The East Peak of Bigelow was named in honor of Myron H. Avery, a Mainer who was chairman of the Appalachian Trail Conference from 1931 to 1952. Avery was elemental in the development of the A.T., particularly in Maine where he all but singlehandedly flagged and cut the route.

The views from Avery rank right up there with Katahdin, and eagle-eyed hikers might spot that particular mountain on a crystal clear day as well as New Hampshire's Mount Washington to the southwest. Both Avery Peak and West Peak feature an above-tree-line alpine area. These areas are home to the rare yellow-nosed vole as well as other interesting small animals. The plants found on these peaks are similar to those found atop Katahdin and New Hampshire's Mount Washington.

In 1976, most of the Bigelow Range (33,000 acres) was saved from development by the people of Maine. A state referendum decided the fate of the Bigelows, and the citizens of Maine voted (by a narrow 3,000-vote margin) to make the Bigelows a wilderness preserve. Seventeen miles of the A.T. (the entire mountain range and a buffer zone) are protected by the preserve.

The Hike
From the parking area on Stratton Brook Pond Road, follow the blue-blazed Firewardens Trail northeast along an old tote road. Ascend gradually for 1.4 miles to the junction with the blue-blazed Horns Pond Trail to the left. Ascend steeply along the Firewardens Trail. The final .75 mile to Bigelow Col is incredibly steep, gaining about 1,300 feet in elevation.

At the floor of Bigelow Col, reach the junction with the A.T. This is also the site of the Myron H. Avery Memorial Lean-to. Hike .5 mile north on the A.T. to the summit of Avery Peak (elevation 4,088 feet). Enroute to the summit, a small spring provides water for the col. From the summit of Avery Peak, hikers will find one of the most outstanding views in the northeast. The Barren-Chairback Range, White Cap and Katahdin can all be seen to the northeast, while the Appalachian Chain, including the Crockers, Saddlebacks, and the Mahoosucs can be viewed stretching away to the southwest. On especially clear days, Mount Washington and the White Mountains of New Hampshire can also be seen to the southwest. The border mountains of Canada are 30 miles to the northwest. Below, and paralleling the Bigelow Range, is Flagstaff Lake. The spillway elevation of the lake is at 1,146 feet.

Return to the col and follow the A.T. .25 mile south to the open summit of the West Peak of Bigelow. At an elevation of 4,150 feet, the views are similar to those found atop Avery Peak.

Return once again to Bigelow Col and follow the Firewardens Trail to Stratton Brook Pond Road.

Trailhead Directions
From the town of Stratton, Maine, on Maine Route 27, drive approximately 4.5 miles east to Stratton Brook Pond Road, which is on the left. Stratton

Brook Pond Road leaves Maine 27 .75 mile north (toward Stratton) of the A.T. crossing. This gravel road intersects the A.T. about 1mile from Route 27. To use the Firewardens Trail, continue another mile further to the trailhead and parking area.

WEST PEAK OF BIGELOW AND THE HORNS

STRENUOUS
10.3 miles roundtrip
8 hours

This loop hike uses very little of the A.T., but it provides the best of both worlds by allowing the hiker a whirlwind tour of the Bigelow Range with spectacular views from both the West Peak of Bigelow and South Horn. A side trail leads .25 mile to the summit of North Horn from the A.T. .5 mile north of Horns Pond. The mountain tarn with its two lean-tos is a good stopping place for a picnic lunch (if you begin your hike early in the day).

The Bigelow Range is probably the most outstanding in Maine. Bigelow is known as "Maine's Second Mountain" next to Katahdin. This long, east-west range consists of six major peaks as well as a number of minor ones. The most spectacular of these are Avery (East) and West Peaks, which are followed closely by the Horns. This hike also uses the Firewardens Trail. Although this trail provides the shortest route to Avery and West Peak, it is also the steepest ascent and descent. The loop with the Horns Pond Trail not only provides a greater enjoyment of the Bigelows but allows a more gradual descent as well.

The East Peak of Bigelow was named in honor of Myron H. Avery, a Mainer who was chairman of the Appalachian Trail Conference from 1931 to 1952. Avery was elemental in the development of the A.T., particularly in Maine where he all but singlehandedly flagged and cut the route.

The views from Avery rank right up there with Katahdin, and eagle-eyed hikers might spot that particular mountain on a crystal clear day as well as New Hampshire's Mount Washington to the southwest. Both Avery Peak and West Peak feature an above-tree-line alpine area. These areas are home to the rare yellow-nosed vole as well as other interesting small animals. The plants found on these peaks are similar to those found atop Katahdin and New Hampshire's Mount Washington.

In 1976, most of the Bigelow Range (33,000 acres) was saved from development by the people of Maine. A state referendum decided the fate of the Bigelows, and the citizens of Maine voted (by a narrow 3,000-vote margin) to make the Bigelows a wilderness preserve. Seventeen miles of the A.T. (the entire mountain range and a buffer zone) are protected by the preserve.

The Hike
From the parking area on Stratton Brook Pond Road, follow the blue-blazed Firewardens Trail northeast along an old tote road. Ascend gradually for 1.4 miles to the junction with the blue-blazed Horns Pond Trail to the left.

Ascend steeply along the Firewardens Trail. The final .75 mile to Bigelow Col is incredibly steep, gaining about 1,300 feet in elevation. At the floor of Bigelow Col, reach the junction with the A.T. This is also the site of the Myron H. Avery Memorial Lean-to.

From the floor of Bigelow Col, take the A.T. south. This will lead you to the open summit of the West Peak of Bigelow after a .25-mile ascent. At an elevation of 4,150 feet, the views are spectacular. The Barren-Chairback Range, White Cap and Katahdin can all be seen to the northeast. The Appalachian chain, including the Crockers, Saddlebacks and the Mahoosucs can be viewed stretching away to the southwest. On especially clear days, Mount Washington and the White Mountains of New Hampshire can also be seen to the southwest. The border mountains of Canada are just over 30 miles to the northwest. Below, and paralleling the Bigelow Range, is Flagstaff Lake. The spillway elevation of the lake is at 1,146 feet.

Upon descending the West Peak, traverse the crest of the range for about 1 mile and then ascend the cone-shaped dome of South Horn. From the small but open summit (elevation 3,831 feet), there is a view of Horns Pond directly below the crest of the range.

From the summit, the trail descends steeply toward the pond. Hike .1 mile to the junction with a side trail that leads .25 mile to the summit of North Horn (elevation 3,815 feet). Hike another .5 mile and reach Horns Pond Lean-tos on the shore of Horns Pond, one of the most outstanding mountain tarns in the state of Maine.

Another .25 mile brings you to the junction of the Horns Pond Trail, which heads south. Follow the Horns Pond Trail, descending moderately for 1 mile before skirting a beaver pond to the south. Continue a gradual descent through hardwoods, following an old logging road for another 1.4 miles to the junction with the Firewardens Trail.

Follow the Firewardens Trail another 1.4 miles to the parking area, the end of this hike.

Trailhead Directions

From the town of Stratton, Maine, on Maine 27, drive approximately 4.5 miles east to Stratton Brook Pond Road, which is on the left. Stratton Brook Pond Road leaves Maine 27 .75 mile north (toward Stratton) of the A.T. crossing. This gravel road intersects the A.T. about 1 mile from Maine 27. To use the Firewardens Trail, continue 1 mile further to the trailhead and parking area.

HORNS POND

STRENUOUS
8.8 miles roundtrip
6 1/2 hours

This hike uses the A.T. to reach the beautiful mountain tarn, Horns Pond. The two lean-tos at Horns Pond make a good stopping place for a picnic lunch if you begin your hike early in the day. This beautiful but rugged climb passes many interesting features, including several small streams, an old loggers pond, and a slab cave system. It also traverses several knobs through dense fir and spruce growth.

Horns Pond is part of the Bigelow Range, which is probably the most outstanding mountain range in Maine. Bigelow is known as "Maine's Second Mountain" next to Katahdin. This long, east-west range consists of six major peaks as well as a number of minor ones. The most outstanding of these are Avery and West Peaks, which are followed closely by the Horns. If you're up for it, you can hike another .5 mile to the .25-mile side trail that leads to the summit of North Horn; or .6 mile to the summit of South Horn. The views from both Horns are spectacular. From South Horn, there is an especially good view of Horns Pond.

In 1976, most of the Bigelow Range (33,000 acres) was saved from development by the people of Maine. A state referendum decided the fate of the Bigelows, and the citizens of Maine voted (by a narrow 3,000-vote margin) to make the Bigelows a wilderness preserve. Seventeen miles of the A.T. (the entire mountain range and a buffer zone) are protected by the preserve.

The Hike
From the parking area on Stratton Brook Pond Road, follow the A.T. north. In the first mile, you will cross Stratton Brook, a logging road, and two small streams. Then begin a moderate ascent up the south slope of the Bigelow Range.

About 1 mile later, pass a dried up logger's pond that still has the remains of an old dam at its outlet, and reach the junction of the Bigelow Range Trail. This trail heads .25 mile west to Cranberry Pond (another pretty mountain tarn) and continues past the pond, passing over the summit of Cranberry Peak (elevation 3,213 feet) and descends to Stratton Village at mile 4.9, .6 mile south of the center of Stratton. From here, turn sharply right and begin to ascend steeply. Hike another .1 mile to an interesting slab cave system.

Reach the crest of the range in another .5 mile, turn eastward, and hike another 1 mile, passing over several knobs thick with spruce and fir. A side trail at the top of a cliff leads to the Lookout, which offers excellent views of Horns Pond below.

Descend steeply through a rocky ravine to the floor of the sag near the pond. Before reaching the Horns Pond Lean-tos, you will reach the junction of the Horns Pond Trail. Continue following the A.T. to the lean-tos.

To return to the parking area and trailhead, follow the A.T. south.

Trailhead Directions
From the town of Stratton, Maine, on Maine 27, drive approximately 4.5 miles east to Stratton Brook Pond Road on the left. Stratton Brook Pond Road leaves Maine 27 .75 mile north (toward Stratton) of the A.T. crossing. This gravel road intersects the A.T. about 1 mile from Maine 27. Use the parking area here to follow the A.T. north to Horns Pond.

PIAZZA ROCK

EASY
3 miles roundtrip
1 1/2 hours

The highlight of this short leg-stretcher is Piazza Rock, a large granite slab that juts out from the side of a cliff. This pleasant woods walk makes a nice afternoon hike. Another side trail, .1 mile past the Piazza Rock Lean-To, leads to The Caves. The Caves were formed by large rocks dropping from the cliffs above.

The Hike

From the trailhead on Maine 4, hike north on the A.T. In .1 mile, the trail crosses Sandy River on a foot bridge. Reach Piazza Rock Lean-to at mile 1.4. The lean-to was built in the 1930s by the CCC. A short side trail beside the shelter leads to Piazza Rock. Another side trail, .1 mile further along the A.T., leads to The Caves.

Return to the parking lot on Maine 4 by following the A.T. south.

Trailhead Directions

The trailhead on Maine 4 is 9 miles south of Rangeley, Maine.

SADDLEBACK MOUNTAIN

STRENUOUS
10.2 miles roundtrip
8 hours

Saddleback Mountain is one of the best day hikes in the state. On this hike, you will find a tremendous rock outcropping, two mountain ponds and an above-treeline climb. Piazza Rock, a large granite slab jutting from the side of a cliff, and the surrounding slab cave system are located on two short side trails. You will skirt the banks of Ethel and Eddy Ponds, two lovely mountain ponds at the base of the Saddleback, and climb the 4,116-foot mountain. The tough climb is well worth the effort because the 360-degree view from the summit is magical.

The Hike

From the trailhead on Maine 4, follow the A.T. north. In .1 mile, you will cross Sandy River on a foot bridge. In another 1.3 miles, the trail reaches Piazza Rock Lean-to. A short side trail beside the shelter leads to the overhanging Piazza Rock. Another side trail, .1 mile further north on the A.T., leads to The Caves, a slab cave system. Both these side trips are well worth the effort, but we suggest that you save them for your return from Saddleback to ensure that you have enough time for the above-treeline section of this day hike.

From the lean-to, hike 2.3 miles to the shore of Ethel Pond. In another .4 mile, you will pass through a boggy section called Mud Pond, and .5 mile past the bog, you will reach the shore of Eddy Pond. Beyond Eddy Pond, the trail ascends steeply up the slopes of Saddleback Mountain. The trail is above treeline for the last 1.1 miles of this hike. Be extremely careful in this section. You are very exposed on the mountain and need to be prepared for severe weather. Make a quick retreat if a storm develops because the mountain offers no protection from the elements.

From the summit of Saddleback Mountain, you can see Bald Mountain, East Kennebago Mountain, Jackson Mountain, the Bigelow Range and many other neighboring mountains and ponds.

To return, follow the A.T. south to Maine 4.

Trailhead Directions
The trailhead on Maine 4 is 9 miles south of Rangeley, Maine.

DUNN NOTCH AND FALLS

EASY
1.6 miles roundtrip
1 hour

This short woods hike leads to the impressive Dunn Notch Falls. The West Branch of the Ellis River drops through the Notch in two waterfalls. The trail crosses the river between the upper and lower falls, both of which can be reached by side trails. The lower falls is a sixty-foot double waterfall dropping sharply into the gorge below.

The Hike
Walk south on the A.T. from East B Hill Road. The trail will cross a brook and enter into Dunn Notch. At mile .75, reach the West Branch of the Ellis River. An old tote road leads down to the bottom of the lower falls. By following the river upstream, you can reach the upper falls.

Return to East B Hill Road by hiking north on the A.T.

Trailhead Directions
The trailhead is 8 miles north of Andover, Maine, on East B Hill Road.

BALDPATE MOUNTAIN

STRENUOUS
7.8 miles roundtrip
6 hours

On this day hike, you will climb out of Grafton Notch to cross the West Peak of Baldpate Mountain (elevation 3,680 feet) with its partially open summit. From West Peak, you will drop sharply into the sag between the mountain's two peaks and then climb to the cairn marking the summit of the East Peak (elevation 3,812 feet). The climb involves areas where you will have to use your hands to negotiate some steep inclines. There is a more than 2,000-foot elevation difference between Grafton Notch and the peaks of Baldpate. The open summit on the East Peak and the fine 360-degree views of the surrounding western Maine mountains are well worth the work it will take to reach the summit.

An optional side trip on your return hike down the mountain will take you to Table Rock. The 1.5-mile trail passes by an overlook with steep cliffs falling away to the notch below. The trail continues on to meet up with the A.T. before it crosses Maine 26.

The Hike
From the trailhead in Grafton Notch, follow the A.T. north. In .1 mile, reach the junction with the Lower Table Rock Trail. Continue along the A.T. for another .75 mile to the Upper Table Rock Trail. Hike 1.4 miles past the Upper Table Rock Trail junction and cross a small stream at the base of Baldpate. For the next .75 mile, climb sharply up the mountain, gaining more than 1,000 feet in elevation. At mile 3, reach the summit of the West Peak of Baldpate, and then drop steeply into the sag between the West and East Peaks. From the West Peak, it is .9 mile to the open summit of the East Peak of Baldpate Mountain.

On your return trip to Grafton Notch, heading south on the A.T., there is an optional side trip to Table Rock, where you will find a tremendous view of the Notch. When you reach the stream at the base of Baldpate, it is 1.4 miles to the Upper Table Rock Trail. Follow the Upper Table Rock Trail to the rock, then continue along the Lower Table Rock Trail to its junction with the A.T. The side trip will add .75 mile to your hike and approximately half an hour to your hiking time. The view is worth the side trip if you have the time.

Trailhead Directions
The parking lot in Grafton Notch State Park is on Maine 26, 12 miles north of US 2 and 7 miles south of the small town of Upton, Maine.

THE EYEBROW

MODERATE
2.2 mile loop
1 1/2 hours

This short but steep hike leads to a viewpoint overlooking the sheer cliffs dropping to Grafton Notch below. The hike uses the A.T. and the Eyebrow Trail to form a loop to this outstanding viewpoint. The hike is rated as moderate because it is relatively short. However, the climb out of the Notch is quite steep, gaining 800 feet in elevation in just over 1 mile.

The Hike
From the trailhead at Grafton Notch on Maine 26, follow the A.T. south. In .1 mile, reach the lower end of the Eyebrow Trail. Continue following the A.T. for 1.1 miles to the junction with the upper end of the Eyebrow Trail. Follow the Eyebrow Trail and reach the Eyebrow in .1 mile. After taking in the fine view, return via the Lower Eyebrow Trail. This section of the trail will lead you back to the A.T. in .75 mile. The Lower Eyebrow Trail joins the A.T. .1 mile from the parking area.

Trailhead Directions
The parking lot in Grafton Notch State Park is on Maine 26, 12 miles north of US 2 and 7 miles south of the small town of Upton, Maine.

OLD SPECK

STRENUOUS
7.6 miles roundtrip
6 hours

This tough hike up out of Grafton Notch will reward you with fine views of the Notch, the Mahoosuc Range and other western Maine mountains. The summit of Old Speck is wooded, but there is an observation tower open to hikers that affords outstanding views. On the return trip, you can take a side trail to the Eyebrow to include another spectacular viewpoint on your dayhike.

The Hike
From the trailhead at Grafton Notch on Maine 26, follow the A.T. south. In .1 mile, reach the lower end of the Eyebrow Trail. Hike another 1.1 miles to the junction with the upper end of the Eyebrow Trail. Continue along the A.T. and reach the junction with the side trail to the summit of Old Speck at mile 3.5. Follow this trail .3 mile to the wooded summit and observation tower on Old Speck. Return to the A.T. and follow it north to Grafton Notch.

An optional side trip on your return is to take the Eyebrow Trail at its upper junction and follow it to its lower terminus on the A.T., just .1 mile from the parking area at Grafton Notch. It is .1 mile to the Eyebrow and another .75 mile from the Eyebrow to the lower terminus on the A.T.

Trailhead Directions
The parking lot in Grafton Notch State Park is on Maine 26, 12 miles north of US 2 and 7 miles south of the small town of Upton, Maine.

SPECK POND

STRENUOUS
9.6 miles roundtrip
7 1/2 hours

At nearly 3,500 feet in elevation, Speck Pond is a beautiful mountain tarn located between Old Speck and Mahoosuc Arm. The pond has a good swimming area near the campsite on the north shore. The Appalachian Mountain Club keeps a maintainer at the trail shelter and campsite, and charges a fee for overnight use. On the return trip, you can take the Upper Eyebrow Trail to the Eyebrow and enjoy spectacular views from the 800-foot cliffs to the Notch below. Be sure to allow plenty of time for your return trip on this long, but beautiful day hike.

The Hike
From the trailhead at Grafton Notch on Maine 26, follow the A.T. south. In .1 mile, reach the lower end of the Eyebrow Trail. Hike another 1.1 miles

to the junction with the upper end of the Eyebrow Trail. Continue along the A.T., and reach the junction with the side trail to the summit of Old Speck at mile 3.5. This trail leads .3 mile to the wooded summit and observation tower on Old Speck. Descend steeply for 1.3 miles to Speck Pond. Return by way of the A.T. north.

An option on the return trip is to follow the Eyebrow trail from its upper junction down to its lower terminus on the A.T., just .1 mile from the parking area at Grafton Notch. It is .1 mile to the Eyebrow from the upper junction and another .75 mile to the lower terminus.

Trailhead Directions
The parking lot in Grafton Notch State Park is on Maine 26, 12 miles north of US 2 and 7 miles south of the small town of Upton, Maine.

NEW HAMPSHIRE

New Hampshire

From the Mahoosuc Range on the Maine border, the Appalachian Trail in New Hampshire heads west over the rugged Carter-Moriah Range and the Wildcat Range to Pinkham Notch. From the Notch, the trail heads up into the Northern Presidential Range with miles of above-treeline trail. This is a very rugged and remote section of trail in the White Mountains National Forest, which attracts thousands of visitors each year. Many visitors underestimate the ruggedness of the terrain. The weather can quickly turn severe in these high elevations: even if the weather down below is expected to be nice, be prepared for the worst when hiking in the Whites. Mount Washington can get snow year round.

As the A.T. crosses the White Mountains, it goes up and over some of the areas best known peaks, including Mount Madison, Mount Washington, Mount Lafayette, Franconia Ridge, Kinsman Mountain and Mount Moosilauke. From the Whites, the trail traverses Mount Cube and Smarts Mountain on the way to Hanover, New Hampshire. The trail goes right through town and passes by Dartmouth College, home of the Dartmouth Outing Club that maintains the trail in this area. The A.T. leaves the state at the Connecticut River.

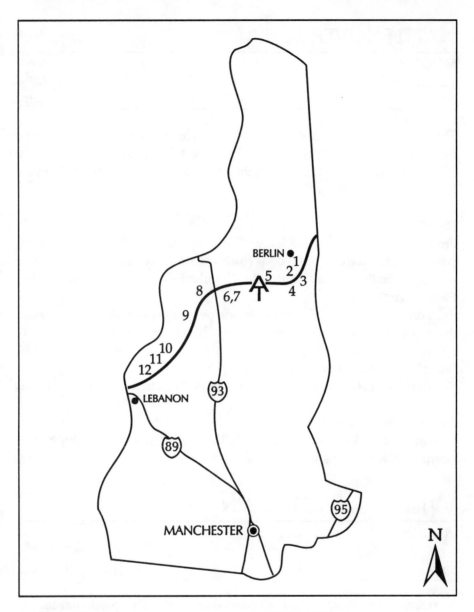

1. Rattle River
2. Wildcat Mountain
3. Lowe's Bald Spot
4. Webster Cliffs
5. Ethan Pond
6. Mt. Lafayette & Mt. Lincoln
7. Mount Liberty
8. Lonesome Lake
9. Mount Moosilauke
10. Mount Cube
11. Smarts Mountain
12. Holts Ledge

RATTLE RIVER

MODERATE
6.0 miles roundtrip
4 hours

This hike follows the Rattle River, along which are a number of pretty picnic spots and swimming holes. The hike takes you first to the Rattle River Shelter. Beyond the shelter, you can take a leisurely, though somewhat steep, stroll along the river.

The Hike
From the parking lot on US 2 near Gorham, follow the Rattle River Trail (also the A.T.) along an old woods road. The trail ascends gradually before passing a lumber campsite at mile .75 mile. Hike another .5 mile to the Rattle River Shelter.

Continue another .75 mile to a fork in the trail. Take the right fork, cross the brook, and begin to ascend steeply. Just over 1 mile later, the A.T. crosses the Rattle River and begins to ascend even more steeply up Mt. Moriah. This is the end of the hike.

To return to the parking lot, follow the A.T. north down the mountain.

Trailhead Directions
To reach the parking lot for the Rattle River Trail, travel 3.8 miles east of Gorham, New Hampshire, on US 2.

WILDCAT MOUNTAIN

STRENUOUS
6 miles roundtrip
5 hours

The Carter-Moriah Range is both rugged and wild. This particular hike is especially exhilarating because it passes an eerily beautiful boggy area along the Ellis River and Lost Pond before ascending Wildcat Mountain. Wildcat features five peaks, but this hike will take you to only two of them—Peaks E and D. Atop Peak E (elevation 4,041 feet), you will pass near the Wildcat Mountain Gondola. In season, the gondola can be taken back down to N.H. 16. Most of the ski trails up here descend to N.H. 16 as well.

The peaks get progressively higher as you head northward. If you feel you have the time and energy, it is another strenuous 1.8 miles to Peak A of Wildcat Mountain (elevation 4,380 feet).

The Hike

From Pinkham Notch, the A.T. follows the Lost Pond Trail along the Ellis River to Lost Pond before ascending the Wildcat Ridge Trail. Following the Lost Pond Trail, you will soon cross a wooden bridge over a small bog. The Square Ledge Trail intersects to the left as the A.T. continues along the Ellis River.

Ascending slightly from the river, pass around the eastern shore of Lost Pond and continue along the outlet stream. Just under 1 mile from Pinkham Notch, turn left onto the Wildcat Ridge Trail. To the right, the Wildcat Ridge Trail leads .1 mile to New Hampshire 16 and Glen Ellis Falls.

Hike another .25 mile and begin the steep ascent of Wildcat Mountain. Use extra care when climbing, especially when reaching the ledges of the mountain. From the lower ledges at mile 1.4, ascend to the middle ledges and pass a side trail to the left that leads to a spring. Reach the upper ledges at mile 2.4.

In another .1 mile, ascend the lower Peak E of Wildcat, and .25 mile later, reach the summit of Peak E (elevation 4,041 feet). The trail swings northward and descends slightly, bypassing the terminal building of the Wildcat Mountain Gondolas. From the terminal building, ascend northeast to Peak D (elevation 4,063 feet), where there are wooden observation platforms with views of Tuckerman Ravine to the left and Huntington Ravine to the right (both on Mount Washington). There are also great views of the northern Presidential Range.

Return via the A.T. (Wildcat Ridge Trail and Lost Pond Trail) to New Hampshire 16 at Pinkham Notch. Or, if the gondolas are in operation, you can ride back down to the highway.

Trailhead Directions

The trail can be reached via New Hampshire 16, 8 miles north of Jackson or 12 miles south of Gorham, New Hampshire.

Lowe's Bald Spot

MODERATE
3.8 miles roundtrip
3 hours

This short day hike leads to an outstanding view of both the northern Presidential Range and the Carter-Moriah Range. The Presidentials are the highest mountain group traversed by the A.T. north of Clingmans Dome in Great Smoky Mountains National Park in North Carolina/Tennessee. For nearly 12 miles, the trail is above treeline and offers spectacular views. The rugged Carter-Moriahs, on the other side of Pinkham Notch, stretch for 20 miles before falling to the Androscoggin River.

This short hike follows the Old Jackson Road before crossing the Mount Washington Auto Road and heading to the Great Gulf Wilderness.

The Hike
From New Hampshire 16 at Pinkham Notch, the A.T. follows the Tuckerman Ravine Trail a short distance west and turns right onto the Old Jackson Road Trail. The Tuckerman Ravine Trail continues ahead to the summit of Mount Washington.

Ascend along the Old Jackson Road Trail and turn left away from the roadbed at mile 1.4, near a brook. Continue to climb steeply to the junction with Raymond Path to the left, which heads southwest across the mountain to the Tuckerman Ravine Trail. Shortly thereafter, cross a brook and reach the junction with the Nelson Crag Trail, which heads left to the Mount Washington Auto Road near the summit of Mount Washington.

At mile 1.7, cross the Mount Washington Auto Road near its 2-milepost. Follow the Madison Gulf Trail into the Great Gulf Wilderness for .1 mile to the side trail to Lowe's Bald Spot. Follow the short side trail to this rocky knob (elevation 2,860 feet), which affords spectacular views of the northern Presidentials and the Carter-Moriah Range.

To return to Pinkham Notch, follow the A.T. via the Madison Gulf, Old Jackson Road and Tuckerman Ravine Trails.

Trailhead Directions
The A.T. at Pinkham Notch can be reached by traveling on New Hampshire 16, 8 miles north of Jackson, New Hampshire, or 12 miles south of Gorham, New Hampshire.

WEBSTER CLIFFS

STRENUOUS
6.6 miles roundtrip
6 hours

The panorama from Webster Cliffs will take your breath away, or what little you have left after the steep ascent from Crawford Notch. Crawford Notch is named in honor of Abel and Ethan Allen Crawford, the father-son team that carved out the first trail to the summit of Mount Washington. After cutting the path in 1819, the Crawfords went on to establish the first hostelries for tourists in the notch that now bears their name.

The notch was discovered by Timothy Nash while hunting moose in 1777. Because there was no pass through the White Mountains at the time (you had to go around them), Nash's discovery made passage through the rugged mountains possible. Almost immediately a road was built that crossed the Saco River (which flows through the notch) thirty-two times. Although passage was difficult, it was easier than traveling all the way around the Whites. The first item to be ported through the new passage was a keg of rum that is said to have ended up considerably lighter when it reached the other end!

In 1825, Samuel Willey opened a hostel in Crawford Notch. The following year, the entire family was killed when a ton of debris parted from the valley wall and demolished the hostel. The slide (which helped determine the geophysical aspect of the notch) did not slow down the activity in the notch. Summer tourists still flocked to the area, and the road remained a prime commercial route. The Willey House site and the Willey Slide are still visible just one mile north of the A.T.'s crossing in the notch.

The Hike
From Crawford Notch on US 302 (elevation 1,277 feet), the A.T. follows the Webster Cliffs Trail east. A short distance from the road, the A.T. crosses a bridge over the Saco River, then climbs steeply, winding through a hardwood forest. At mile 1.8, reach Webster Cliffs. For the next 1.5 miles, the trail follows the cliffs to the summit of Mount Webster (elevation 3,910 feet).

To return to Crawford Notch, follow the A.T./Webster Cliffs Trail south to US 302.

Trailhead Directions
The A.T. at Crawford Notch can be reached via US 302 by traveling 8 miles north of Bartlett, or 10 miles south of Twin Mountain, New Hampshire.

ETHAN POND

STRENUOUS
7 miles roundtrip
5 hours

Located along the edges of the Pemigewasset Wilderness, this short hike takes you across a low point in the Willey Range (elevation 2,907 feet) before reaching Ethan Pond. Although the elevation gain is relatively gradual, there is still a gain of more than 1,500 feet in the 3.5 mile trip to Ethan Pond. This elevation gain alone makes the trip a notch over moderate when it comes to the energy expended.

Pretty Ethan Pond is home to both moose and bear. Many have been spotted there so keep an eye out. Tamarack, also called the Eastern Larch, line the shores of the pond.

The hike begins at Crawford Notch, named in honor of Abel and Ethan Allen Crawford, the father-son team that carved out the first trail to the summit of Mount Washington. After cutting the path in 1819, the Crawfords went on to establish the first hostelries for tourists in the notch that now bears their name.

The notch was discovered by Timothy Nash while hunting moose in 1777. Because there was no pass through the White Mountains at the time (you had to go around them), Nash's discovery made passage through the rugged mountains possible. Almost immediately a road was built that crossed the Saco River (which flows through the notch) thirty-two times. Although passage was difficult, it was easier than traveling all the way around the Whites. The first item to be ported through the new passage was a keg of rum that is said to have ended up considerably lighter when it reached the other end!

In 1825, Samuel Willey opened a hostel in Crawford Notch. The following year, the entire family was killed when a ton of debris parted from the valley wall and demolished the hostel. The slide (which helped determine the geophysical aspect of the notch) did not slow down the activity in the notch. Summer tourists still flocked to the area, and the road remained a prime commercial route. The Willey House site and the Willey Slide are still visible just one mile north of the A.T.'s crossing in the notch.

The Hike
From US 302 in Crawford Notch, follow the A.T. south up Willey House Station Road. Ascend the path to the right of the parking area, cross over railroad tracks, and take the Ethan Pond Trail up into the woods.

At mile .5, reach the intersection of the Arethusa-Ripley Falls Trail, which heads left .4 mile to Ripley Falls, 2.5 miles to Arethusa Falls, and 3.8 miles back to US 302. Continue along the A.T., and ascend rather steeply then more gradually for .5 mile. At mile 1.6, reach the junction with the Kedron Flume Trail, which descends steeply right to the Willey House on US 302.

In another .25 mile, the A.T./Ethan Pond Trail turns left and the Willey Range Trail continues straight ahead. Continue on the A.T. and reach the height of the land in .25 mile. Begin a slight descent along a former logging road, and just over 1 mile later, reach the side trail to Ethan Pond.

To return to Crawford Notch, follow the A.T./Ethan Pond Trail north.

Trailhead Directions
To reach the A.T. at Crawford Notch, take US 302, 8 miles north of Bartlett, or 10 miles south of Twin Mountain, New Hampshire.

Mt. Lafayette and Mt. Lincoln

STRENUOUS
8.6 miles roundtrip
9 hours

This day hike is in one of the more spectacular sections of the Whites. It uses very little of the A.T., but it is definitely an exception to the general rule. Both Mount Lafayette and Mount Lincoln are above treeline, reaching over 5,000 feet in elevation—treeline occurs on Franconia Ridge at approximately 4,200 feet. Above this elevation, only krummholz (stunted spruce) and other alpine vegetation exist. Because this vegetation is extremely vulnerable to erosion (caused in a large part by the tramping of feet), please remain on the established treadway.

Beginning at Profile Clearing on US 3, this day hike uses the Greenleaf

Trail as well as the A.T. Profile Clearing is a part of Franconia Notch State Park, which encompasses The Basin, a glacial pothole twenty feet in diameter (it was carved in granite at the base of a waterfall more than 25,000 years ago); The Old Man of the Mountains, a forty-foot stone profile of a man's face formed by five ledges at Cannon Cliffs that stands about 1,200 feet above Profile Lake; and The Flume, a natural chasm more than 800 feet long with walls of granite sixty to seventy feet high and twelve to twenty feet wide.

The Hike

At US 3 at Profile Clearing, take the Greenleaf Trail for 2.2 miles to Greenleaf Hut. From the hut, hike another 1.1 miles to reach the summit of Mount Lafayette (elevation 5,249 feet). You will see the remains of the summit house foundation just below the summit.

From the summit of Mount Lafayette, it is another 1 mile to the top of Mount Lincoln (elevation 5,089 feet). The walk along this ridge is absolutely spectacular, but it can be dangerous in inclement weather. The ridge is exposed to the full force of storms, which can occur both suddenly and violently. Conditions can include hurricane-force winds and freezing temperatures (even in the summer). Be prepared. Bring along rain gear and a warm coat or sweater in your daypack for emergencies. Head for Greenleaf Hut if the weather turns threatening.

Return to US 3 at Profile Clearing via the Greenleaf Trail.

Trailhead Directions

Profile Clearing is about 11 miles north of North Woodstock, New Hampshire, on US 3, and approximately 5 miles south of Franconia, New Hampshire, on US 3.

MOUNT LIBERTY

STRENUOUS
8.2 miles roundtrip
7 hours

This hike involves a tough climb to the summit of Mount Liberty (elevation 4,459 feet). You will be richly rewarded at the peak with a commanding view of Mount Lincoln, Mount Lafayette, the rest of Franconia Ridge and other peaks in the White Mountains. On days when there seems to be a single-file line of hikers heading up from Profile Clearing to Mounts Lafayette and Lincoln, this hike offers a chance to get away from the heaviest crowds. The hike uses the A.T. until you are .25 mile from the summit. An optional return route takes you to the summit of Mount Flume and returns to US 3 via the side trail to the Flume.

The Hike

From the parking area at US 3 in Franconia Notch, take the mile-long Whitehouse Trail to its junction with the A.T. Follow the A.T. north. In .4 mile, reach the junction with the Flume side trail. Continue on the A.T., climbing sharply for 2.4 miles up the mountain to Liberty Springs Campsite. Water is available from the spring located near the trail at the campsite.

From the campsite, the trail climbs steeply for .4 mile to the junction with the Franconia Ridge Trail. Turn right on to the Ridge Trail and reach the summit of Mount Liberty in .25 mile. After enjoying the views from Liberty, hike the .25 mile back down to the A.T. and return to your car via that trail.

The optional return is to continue on the Franconia Ridge Trail for .9 mile to the summit of Mount Flume (elevation 4,327 feet). From the summit of Mount Flume, follow the Flume side trail for 3.8 miles down the mountain to its junction with the A.T. The Flume side trail descent off Mount Flume is quite steep for the first .5 mile and then eases up as you reach Flume Brook. From the junction with the A.T., it is .4 mile south to the trailhead at US 3. This return route adds 2.1 miles to your roundtrip, but you get to climb Mount Flume and enjoy a nice walk along Flume Brook.

Trailhead Directions

The parking area in Franconia Notch is just north of the New Hampshire State Park Flume Complex, which is just over 5 miles north of North Woodstock on US 3. From the parking area, take the mile-long Whitehouse Trail to the A.T.

LONESOME LAKE

MODERATE
7.6 miles roundtrip
4 1/2 hours

You will cross over two beautiful brooks—Whitehouse and Cascade—on this hike to Lonesome Lake. Set against the backdrop of Profile Mountain, the lake itself is a mountain tarn that sits high on the side of Cannon Mountain.

The elevation change from the trailhead to the lake is over 1,000 feet, but the trail is well-graded and the climb is moderate. Lonesome Lake can make for a good hike with children old enough for a trail that offers some challenges along the way.

The Hike

From the parking area on US 3, follow the mile-long Whitehouse Trail to its junction with the A.T. Follow the A.T. south and cross under US 3. Hike .25 mile to Whitehouse Brook, which you cross on rocks. Hike another 1.1 miles to the junction with the Basin-Cascades Trail. Continue to follow the A.T., which will cross and then follow alongside of Cascade Brook as you continue to climb up to Lonesome Lake.

From the Basin-Cascades Trail, it is .5 mile to the junction with the Kinsman Pond Trail. Continue to follow the A.T. alongside Cascade Brook, hiking another .9 mile to Lonesome Lake. Lonesome Lake Hut is .1 mile beyond the lake. The Appalachian Mountain Club operates the hut, where water is available and some refreshments are sold.

The return hike is north on the A.T. to the Whitehouse Trail, which you follow to the parking area on US 3.

Trailhead Directions

The parking lot is located just over 5 miles north of North Woodstock, New Hampshire on US 3. If you are coming from North Woodstock, the parking area is just past the New Hampshire State Park Flume Complex.

Mount Moosilauke

STRENUOUS
6.4 miles roundtrip
7 hours

If you look up the words "big" and "beautiful" in your thesaurus, you find dozens of adjectives to describe Mount Moosilauke, which means "high bald place" in the language of the Pemigewasset Indians. But all of those words fall short in describing this imposing bald mountain that stands over the southwest corner of the White Mountains.

A carriage road leading to the open summit of Moosilauke was built in the mid-1800s. It led to the Prospect House, a hotel on top of the massif. The hotel was bought by Dartmouth College in 1920 and maintained as a hostel until 1942, when the old hotel burned down. The road is long since abandoned and the summit is free from development, but Mount Moosilauke still boasts the commanding view that attracted visitors a century ago.

This is a challenging hike, and should not be taken lightly. There is a 1,000-foot gain in elevation for every mile of this hike. Allow ample time for your return trip because the descent can be tricky at times.

The Hike

From the trailhead at Kinsman Notch on New Hampshire 112, follow the A.T. north. The trail climbs gradually for the first .5 mile where, to the right of the trail, you will see the lowest of a series of falls on Beaver Brook. At this point, the trail begins its very steep climb out of Kinsman Notch.

For most of the next .5 mile, you will be alongside, or at some points almost in, Beaver Brook as you climb up to the col between Mount Blue and Mount Jim, which you reach at mile 1.4 . From the col, begin climbing the side of Mount Blue, follow the trail alongside that peak as you skirt Jobildunk Ravine to the left of the trail, and reach a second col in .5 mile. Climb another .9 mile to the open summit of Mount Moosilauke. Ruins of the old hotel are visible around the summit. The old carriage road can be seen leading to the South Peak of Moosilauke. There are outstanding views in all directions, particularly to the northeast where the peaks of the White Mountains are prominent.

The return hike is back down the A.T. to Kinsman Notch.

Trailhead Directions
The trail crosses New Hampshire 112 just over 6 miles west of North Woodstock, New Hampshire. Parking is available at the trailhead.

Mount Cube

STRENUOUS
6.8 miles roundtrip
6 hours

From the southern summit of Mount Cube, you can see the Connecticut River Valley and the solitary summits of Smarts Mountain and Mt. Ascutney. A short side trail takes you to the northern peak of Mount Cube where you will find views of Mount Moosilauke and the White Mountains from its open ledges. This hike also features a short stroll along a New Hampshire bog before it ascends over mixed terrain, passing several brooks along the way. There is an elevationgain of nearly 2,000 feet, which makes this hike rather tough.

The Hike
The hike begins at New Hampshire 25A, near Upper Baker Pond. A short distance from a highway bridge, enter the woods on the A.T. at the southern side of the highway. After crossing a small swamp, begin to ascend on abandoned logging roads. At mile .25, you will cross a gravel logging road and continue your ascent.

Hike another 1.5 miles, cross a log bridge over Brackett's Brook, and start your ascent of Mount Cube via switchbacks. Hike another 1.5 miles to the saddle between the summits of North and South Cube.

A short side trail leads to the summit of North Cube where you will find open ledges and outstanding views of the Whites. The A.T. continues to the left and soon reaches the summit of South Cube (elevation 2,911 feet) where you will find views of the Connecticut River Valley, Smarts Mountain and Mt. Ascutney.

Return via the A.T., heading north.

Trailhead Directions
The A.T. at New Hampshire 25A can be reached by traveling about 4 miles west of Wentworth, New Hampshire, and 20 miles west of Interstate 93.

SMARTS MOUNTAIN

MODERATE
7.6 miles roundtrip
6 hours

This beautiful hike over open rocky ledges leads to the summit of Smarts Mountain where you will find wonderful views of the New Hampshire countryside.

The Hike

From the parking lot on Lyme-Dorchester Road, you will immediately begin your ascent of Lambert Ridge. (The Smarts Mountain Ranger Trail, which leads right to the summit of Smarts, is an alternative to make the hike a loop hike, and is about the same distance as returning by the A.T.)

Hike about .75 mile to the first series of open ledges on the spine of Lambert Ridge. One mile later, descend Lambert Ridge, cross a stream, and begin your ascent of Smarts Mountain. Hike another 1.5 miles to the junction of the Smarts Mountain Ranger Trail. These two trails join and you will continue on them until you reach the summit. In about .25 mile, the trail makes a sharp right and ascends steeply to the summit.

Pass the short side trail leading to the Smarts Mountain tent site in .1 mile. Water is available from an intermittent spring just beyond the trail junction. Hike another .1 mile, and pass just east of the summit of Smarts Mountain (elevation 3,240 feet). The Smarts Mountain Ranger Trail ends here.

From here, you can also see the Firewarden's Cabin, now maintained as a shelter by the Dartmouth Outing Club. More water is available from the Mike Murphy Spring, .1 mile north of this cabin on a blue-blazed side trail.

Return via the A.T. or the Smarts Mountain Ranger Trail.

Trailhead Directions

To reach the Lyme-Dorchester Road and its northern junction with the A.T. and the Smarts Mountain Ranger Trail, start at Lyme on New Hampshire 10 and travel 3.2 miles to a fork and the road's first junction with the A.T. Follow the northern (left) fork of the road to the parking lot at the A.T./ Smarts Mountain Ranger Trail junction.

HOLTS LEDGE

MODERATE
3 miles roundtrip
2-3 hours

Holts Ledge is the site of a successful peregrine falcon restoration project. Every year since 1988, young falcons have been seen launching themselves from the ledges as they take their first flight. Of the seven pairs of nesting peregrines in New Hampshire, one pair has taken up residence at Holts Ledge.

But, the peregrines are a seriously endangered species that will disappear if humans intrude. The success of a cooperative program involving the Appalachian Trail Conference, the Dartmouth Outing Club, the New Hampshire Audobon Society, the New Hampshire Fish and Game Commission, and the U.S. Fish and Wildlife Service depends on hikers heeding the signs posted during mating season (early spring to mid-summer). Please help protect the peregrine falcons that have been reintroduced to the area after decades of absence by staying behind the fences. If you're lucky you may spot one of these magnificent raptors.

The Hike
From the Lyme-Dorchester Road (at its first junction with the A.T.), head southwest along the A.T. and begin a gradual ascent through the woods. Hike .9 mile to the side trail that leads about .25 mile to the Trapper John Shelter—named for that fictional Dartmouth student from the television series M*A*S*H.

The trail continues to climb gradually, eventually crossing a small (intermittent) brook before it ascends more steeply along several small ridges. At mile 1.4, reach the junction with the .1-mile side trail that leads to the viewpoint at Holts Ledge.

Return via the side trail to the A.T. and follow the A.T. north back to Lyme-Dorchester Road.

Trailhead Directions
To reach the Lyme-Dorchester Road and its southern junction with the A.T. at the Dartmouth Skiway, start at Lyme on New Hampshire 10 and travel 3.2 miles to a fork and the road's first junction with the A.T.

VERMONT

VERMONT

From the Connecticut River at the Vermont/New Hampshire border, the Appalachian Trail passes from east to west for over forty miles. Crossing through lowland hardwood forests and climbing over steep hills dotted with pastures and fields, the A.T. joins the Long Trail at Sherburne Pass where it heads 101 miles south to the Vermont/Massachusetts border.

The northern section of the trail in Vermont passes through an area once populated by many farms. The area from the Connecticut River to Sherburne Pass features cleared hills, pastures, ravines, steep hills and patches of timber. Stone walls, cellar holes and other remnants of the farms that once dominated this area can still be seen. The area is now reverting to forest.

At Sherburne Pass, the Long Trail, which joined the A.T. at the Vermont/Massachusetts border, heads north another 160 miles or so to Canada. The A.T. picks up the Long Trail here and follows it south. The A.T climbs the slopes of Killington and Pico Peaks of the Coolidge Range, reaching its highest point in Vermont just below Killington Peak (elevation 4,235 feet). Once the trail passes through the Coolidge Range, its descends once again to rolling hills and farmlands, and crosses Clarendon Gorge on a suspension bridge before climbing back up into the Green Mountains.

From here, the A.T. follows the ridge of the Green Mountains, passing several mountain ponds (Little Rock Pond, Griffith Lake and Stratton Pond). The trail also crosses several peaks, including Peru Peak, Spruce Peak and Stratton Mountain. The latter is said to be the birthplace of the A.T. Here, Benton MacKaye first envisioned a trail along the Appalachian Mountains.

From Stratton, the trail continues on to Glastenbury Mountain before descending toVermont 9 near Bennington, Vermont. Then the trail climbs to follow a rolling ridge for 14 miles until it meets the Vermont/Massachusetts border. The border is not near a road crossing. It is another 4 miles to Massachusetts 2 in North Adams.

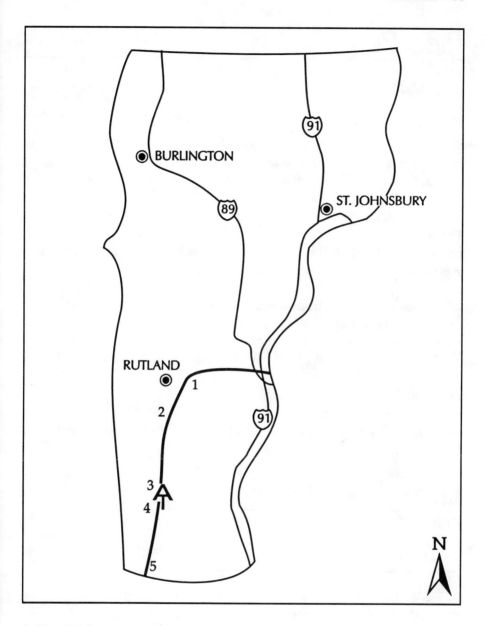

1. Pico Peak
2. Little Rock Pond
3. Prospect Rock
4. Stratton Mountain
5. Harmon Hill

Pico Peak

STRENUOUS
5.8 miles roundtrip
5 hours

Ski trails will never be far away as you climb up to Pico Peak. The summit is shared with the Pico Peak Ski Resort chair lift, but this hike rewards you for your effort in climbing the 3,957-foot peak with fine views from the skiway and summit.

The Hike
From the trailhead on US 4 in Sherburne Pass, follow the A.T. south. You will pass by a side trail to the Pico alpine slide. Continue following the A.T. uphill and reach Pico Camp, a cabin maintained as a hiker shelter, at mile 2.5. Water is available from a small spring a short distance beyond the shelter. Behind the camp, the steep blue-blazed Pico Link Trail climbs the remaining .4 mile to the summit of Pico Peak.

Return by way of the Pico Link Trail and the A.T. to Sherburne Pass.

Trailhead Directions
The trail crosses Sherburne Pass, on US 4, 10.3 miles east of Rutland at the Inn at Long Trail. The restaurant and bar at the Inn are recommended, if you have the time.

Little Rock Pond

EASY
5.8 miles roundtrip
3 hours

This is the best day hike on the A.T. in Vermont. The gentle climb from the road to the pond is a great way to get out and stretch your legs. The trail runs alongside Little Black Brook for much of the hike, and many small waterfalls and pools are visible from the trail.

The clear, cold water of the pond reflects Green Mountain rising above it on the opposite shore. This is a popular day hike, particularly in the fall (the foliage around the pond is breathtaking at its peak). If you want to have any solitude, try this hike during the week or leave the trailhead by 10 A.M. to beat the crowds.

This can be hiked as a roundtrip, or by using the Green Mountain Trail, you can hike a 7.5-mile loop.

The Hike

From the trailhead at the parking lot on USFS 10 (Danby-Landgrove Road), hike north on the A.T. Reach the southern end of Little Rock Pond at mile 2. The trail skirts the eastern shore of the pond for the next .4 mile. At the northern end of the pond, the Green Mountain Trail, which can be used to create a 7.5-mile loop, turns left off of the A.T. Even if you don't care to follow this trail back to the parking lot, you may want to follow it around the pond. It joins the LittleRock Pond Loop Trail, which can be followed back to the southern end of the pond. Return by way of the A.T.

If you decide to follow the Green Mountain Trail, climb 1 mile up the ridge to the summit of Green Mountain (elevation 2,500 feet). Continue following the trail for another 4.1 miles as it traverses and descends the ridge to USFS 10, about .1 mile west of the parking lot at the A.T. trailhead.

Trailhead Directions

The A.T. crosses Danby-Landgrove Road (USFS 10) 3.5 miles east of US 7 in Danby, Vermont.

PROSPECT ROCK

MODERATE
9.8 miles roundtrip
6 hours

This long day hike features outstanding views of the Dorset Valley, Manchester and Mount Equinox.

The Hike

From the parking area on Vermont 11/30, cross the road, ascend the highway bank, and enter the woods (also a boulder field). Hike nearly half a mile and cross a stream and the old, overgrown Vermont 11/30. Hike another .25 mile, cross another stream, and begin to ascend steeply.

Almost 1 mile after beginning your hike, you will pass two vistas (one to the south and one to the northwest), reach a ridgetop, and descend down a narrow ridge through a hardwood forest. Hike another .9 mile, cross an old woods road and a small brook, and ascend west and then south.

At mile 2.2, reach the junction with a side trail that leads a short distance to Spruce Peak (elevation 2,060 feet). At this side trail, head left along the A.T. for another .5 mile to the side trail to Spruce Peak Shelter. Water is available from a spring just south of the shelter, which is .1 mile off the trail.

Hike another .4 mile, cross a stream in a small gully, turn sharply left, and ascend the ridge. Reach the highpoint on the western flank of the ridge in .25 mile, continue south for just over 1 mile, cross a small stream, and descend.

At mile 4.9, reach the side trail that leads a short distance to Prospect Rock (elevation 2,079 feet), which affords magnificent views of the Dorset Valley, Manchester and Mount Equinox.

Return to the parking area by retracing your footsteps north on the A.T.

Trailhead Directions
The trail crossing at Vermont 11/30 is 5.5 miles east of Manchester Center and 4.4 miles west of Peru.

STRATTON MOUNTAIN

MODERATE	
6.8 miles roundtrip	
6 hours	

The peak of Stratton Mountain (elevation 3,936 feet) is said to be the birthplace of the A.T. The views from this mountain sparked the idea of an eastern continental trail in the mind of Benton MacKaye. Sitting in a tree, admiring the panorama, MacKaye said the experience left him with the impression that he was "atop the world, with a sort of planetary feeling." MacKaye later went on to publish his concept of a continual footpath along the Appalachian Mountains. The idea ignited interest, and by 1937 his dream was on its way to fulfillment.

The recent re-routing of the trail over Stratton Mountain provides hikers with a beautiful climb and outstanding views of the Green Mountains and surrounding countryside. From the observation tower at the summit, you can see Somerset Reservoir and Mount Pisgah to the south, Glastenbury Mountain to the southwest, the Taconics to the west, Ascutney Mountain to the northeast, and Mount Monadnock to the southeast (the latter two in New Hampshire).

Less than 1 mile away and to the north, the North Peak of Stratton and the Stratton Chair Lift can be reached by a side trail. The Starship XII gondola operates daily (weather permitting) from June through early October.

The Hike

From the parking area on Arlington-West Wardsboro Road (also signed as Kelley Stand Road), follow the A.T. into the woods. After passing a beaver pond, you will begin to ascend gradually, crossing an old woods road.

At mile 1.1, pass by cellar holes and the well of an old farmstead. In another .25 mile, cross a dirt road and begin your ascent of the southwestern ridge of Stratton Mountain. The trail follows switchbacks and reaches the bench below the summit of Little Stratton Mountain in another .75 mile. The trail follows the bench to a col between Little Stratton and Stratton Mountains, ascending steeply by switchbacks.

At mile 2.8, pass a piped spring, and at mile 3.4, reach the tower at the summit. After the spring, keep an eye out for an outstanding view of Grout Pond to the south. During the season (May through October), a caretaker with Green Mountain Club lives in the cabin atop Stratton. The caretaker is often available to provide hikers with information about the area.

Return via the A.T., heading south to the parking area.

Trailhead Directions

The A.T. crossing at Arlington-West Wardsboro Road is 13.2 miles east of Arlington, Vermont.

HARMON HILL

MODERATE
3.4 miles roundtrip
3-4 hours

The summit of Harmon Hill affords beautiful views of the picturesque college town of Bennington, Vermont. Mount Anthony can be seen to the west, and there is also a view of the Battle Monument, which commemorates the Battle of Bennington fought on August 16, 1777. There are also limited views to the north of Bald Mountain and Glastenbury Mountain.

The Hike
The hike begins at the Bennington-Brattleboro Highway (Vermont 9). From the highway (elevation 1,360 feet), climb steeply up rock and log steps for nearly .5 mile. At mile .6, head southwest and begin to ascend more gradually.

At mile 1.5, you will enter a clearing, and about .25 mile later, reach the open summit of Harmon Hill (elevation 2,325 feet). From here, retrace your steps back to the Bennington-Brattleboro Highway.

Trailhead Directions
The trail crossing at Bennington-Brattleboro Highway (Vermont 9) is 5.1 miles east of Bennington and 2.8 miles west of Woodford.

MASSACHUSETTS

MASSACHUSETTS

The Appalachian Trail enters Massachusetts 4 miles north of a road crossing (Massachusetts 2 in North Adams), descending along the rocky ridge of East Mountain. From North Adams, the trail continues up Prospect Mountain Ridge and over Mount Williams and Mount Fitch to the summit of Mount Greylock, the highest point in Massachusetts (elevation 3,491 feet).

From Mount Greylock, the A.T. descends to Cheshire, heads over to Dalton, and climbs the Berkshire Highlands. The trail traverses High Top and passes by Finerty Pond before entering October Mountain State Forest. After crossing US 20 at Greenwater Pond, the A.T. continues to Goose Pond and descends into the Tyringham Valley. From Tyringham, the A.T. enters the Beartown State Forest, skirting Benedict Pond.

From here, the trail heads southwest into East Mountain State Forest, crosses over Warner and June Mountains, and descends to the Housatonic River. The last miles of the A.T. in Massachusetts cross the valley to the Taconic Range, climb Mount Everett and Mount Race, pass beautiful Bear Rock Falls, and descend to the Connecticut border in Sages Ravine.

The many scenic ponds, such as Upper Goose, Benedict and Finerty, are perhaps the dominant feature of the A.T.'s 89 miles in Massachusetts.

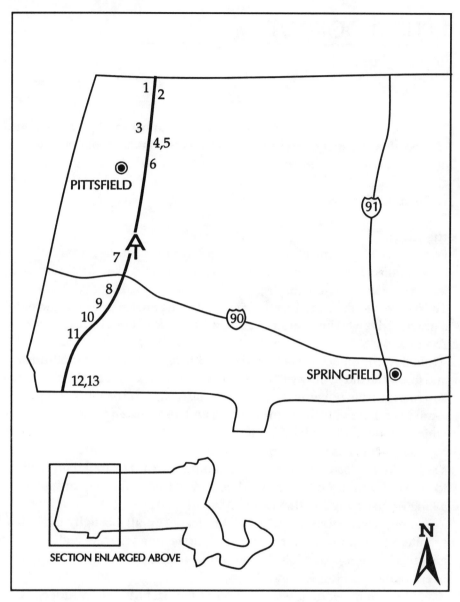

SECTION ENLARGED ABOVE

N

1. Eph's Lookout
2. Mount Prospect
3. The Cobbles
4. The Cobbles and Gore Pond
5. Gore Pond
6. Warner Hill
7. Finerty Pond

8. Upper Goose Pond
9. Cobble Hill
10. Benedict Pond and The Ledges
11. East Mountain
12. Jug End
13. Jug End and Mount Everett

EPH'S LOOKOUT

MODERATE
6.6 miles roundtrip
5 hours

This hike will take you to a quartzite ridge known as Eph's Lookout. Named after Colonel Ephraim Williams, the lookout has wonderful views of Williamstown, Mount Greylock and the Berkshires. In his will, Williams changed the name of West Hoosac to Williamstown and established the Williams College as a free school.

The Hike
From the A.T. crossing at Massachusetts 2 in North Adams, cross over the B&M Railroad and Hoosic River on a concrete and steel footbridge. At Massachusetts Avenue, turn right and follow the road for about .25 mile. The trail leaves the paved road, turns west along Sherman Brook and onto a gravel driveway just before Sherman Brook goes under Massachusetts Avenue.

Follow the gravel driveway a short distance, pass over two footbridges, and follow an old spillway that releases water from a circular dam. At mile .6, a high voltage powerline crosses the trail next to the brook. For the next .4 mile, climb steadily through hemlocks and turn onto an old logging road, which you will follow for .25 mile.

At mile 1.6, pass Pete's Spring to the right and reach the junction with a side trail that leads to a designated camping area. The trail then returns to the bank of the brook, follows old logging roads for .25 mile, and ascends a long ridge covered with patches of laurel.

At mile 2.4, turn sharply west, climb steeply uphill through a jumble of granite, marble and quartz, climb a couple of steep and narrow switchbacks, and reach the top of a bluff. The bluff faces east and has a campsite overlooking the Hoosic Range.

Hike .1 mile along a wide section of the East Mountain Ridge, pass around the north side of a fragile, mossy pond, and climb to the top of an open area with quartzite cobble. Reach the junction with the Pine Cobble Trail in .1 mile. There is a panoramic view a short distance south on the Pine Cobble Trail.

Continue along the A.T. and reach a dip in the ridge in .25 mile. In another .25 mile, reach the destination of the day hike—Eph's Lookout, a fine overlook with views of the Berkshires, Williamstown, Mount Greylock, the Taconic Range and the Hoosic Valley.

To return to the parking area, follow the A.T. south to Massachusetts 2.

Trailhead Directions
The trail crossing at Massachusetts 2 is in North Adams, Massachusetts. Parking is available at the Greylock Community Club, a short distance east of the A.T. crossing. Let someone at the club know that you are leaving your vehicle.

MOUNT PROSPECT

MODERATE
5.6 miles roundtrip
4 hours

The highlights of this day hike include views of Williamstown, the Taconic Ridge, Eph's Lookout and the Lower Pine Cobble.

The Hike
From the A.T. crossing at Massachusetts 2 in North Adams, follow the A.T. south on Phelps Avenue. There are fine views of Mount Williams to the left and Prospect Ridge to the right. Reach the junction of Catherine Street at mile .4. Behind you are views of the border hills of Eph's Lookout and the lower Pine Cobble.

In .1 mile, after a steep climb up a private driveway, the trail turns sharply away from the house and heads down to cross a brook on a bridge. In another .25 mile, a local trail turns left as the A.T. heads right. The trail soon crosses a small brook and begins its ascent up the ridge.

In another .25 mile, the trail crosses Pattison Road and heads into a spruce plantation on the south side of the road. This area is part of the North Adams Watershed.

After crossing the watershed access road at mile 1.7, the A.T. climbs

steeply to the boundary of the Mount Greylock State Reservation. Here, the trail turns west into a hemlock grove and climbs the long, steep ridge up Mount Prospect.

Ascending steeply through northern hardwoods, you will come to a view of Williamstown and the Taconic Range at mile 2.8. This is also the junction of the Mount Prospect Trail, the destination point for this day hike.

Follow the A.T. north back to Massachusetts 2.

Trailhead Directions
The trail crossing is at Massachusetts 2 is in North Adams, Massachusetts. Parking is available at the Greylock Community Club, 100 yards east of the A.T. crossing. Let someone at the club know that you are leaving your vehicle.

THE COBBLES

MODERATE
2.8 miles roundtrip
3 hours

The main attraction of this short day hike is the view of Cheshire and the valley from the Cobbles. The white quartz that makes up the Cobbles was beach sand 550 million years ago when this area was on the edge of the ocean.

Most of this section of the A.T. was obtained from the Crane family of Dalton. The Crane Company is the manufacturer of the paper used for U.S. currency. The company runs a currency museum in Dalton.

The Hike
Start at the Post Office on Church Street (park where you want—and can— in the town of Cheshire). On your right, you will see a replica of the press used to make Cheshire Cheese in the 1800s. Heading south on the A.T., you will cross railroad tracks in .1 mile and then a bridge over the Hoosic River. After crossing the bridge, turn right at a fork in the road.

In another .1 mile, you will turn right on Furnace Hill Road, a residential street. After another .25 mile, you will turn left off Furnace Hill Road near the entrance of a private driveway.

For the next .75 mile, you will ascend through a hardwood forest, crossing motorcycle and logging trails. You will then arrive at the side trail to the north Cobble immediately after passing under a cliff. The A.T. reaches the top of the southernmost Cobble .25 mile later. Here, there is a USGS bronze marker set into the edge. This is the destination of the hike.

From here, retrace your steps north on the A.T. back to Cheshire.

Trailhead Directions
From Massachusetts 8 in Cheshire, turn onto Church Street. The Post Office and St. Mary of the Assumption Catholic Church are along the A.T.

THE COBBLES AND GORE POND

MODERATE
6.6 miles roundtrip
5 hours

The main attraction of this short day hike is the view of Cheshire and the valley from the Cobbles and the scenic Gore Pond. The white quartz that makes up the Cobbles was beach sand 550 million years ago when this area was on the edge of the ocean.

Most of this section of the A.T. was obtained from the Crane family of Dalton. The Crane Company is the manufacturer of the paper used for U.S. currency. The company runs a currency museum in Dalton.

The Hike
Start at the Post Office on Church Street (park where you want—and can—in the town of Cheshire). On your right, you will see a replica of the press used to make Cheshire Cheese in the 1800s. Heading south on the A.T., you will cross railroad tracks in .1 mile and then a bridge over the Hoosic River. After crossing the bridge, turn right at a fork in the road.

In another .1 mile, you will turn right on Furnace Hill Road, a residential street. After another .25 mile, you will turn left off Furnace Hill Road near the entrance of a private driveway.

For the next .75 mile, you will ascend through a hardwood forest, crossing motorcycle and logging trails. You will then arrive at the side trail to the north Cobble immediately after passing under a cliff. The A.T. reaches the top of the southernmost Cobble .25 mile later. Here, there is a USGS bronze marker set into the edge.

Continue along the A.T. In .5 mile, turn east near the stone boundary marker for Dalton-Cheshire. The trail crosses an old, grassy logging road and continues for 1.3 miles, heading gradually uphill, crossing old logging roads, and eventually reaching the summit at an overgrown pasture. From here, the trail begins its descent to Gore Pond, reaching the outlet in about .5 mile. There is a logging road here that provides access to the west side of the pond, the destination of this hike.

Return north to Cheshire via the A.T.

Trailhead Directions
From Massachusetts 8 in Cheshire, turn onto Church Street. The Post Office and St. Mary of the Assumption Catholic Church are along the Appalachian Trail.

Gore Pond

MODERATE
8.4 miles roundtrip
5 hours

Pretty Gore Pond is the destination of this day hike, which begins in Dalton, Massachusetts. Most of this section of the A.T. was obtained from the Crane family of Dalton. The Crane Company is the manufacturer of the paper used for U.S. currency. The company runs a currency museum in Dalton.

The Hike
The hike begins on Gulf Road. You will soon turn right into the woods and parallel the road. For the next 3.3 miles, the A.T. ascends and descends many ridges while skirting the wet areas between them. The A.T. follows the Dalton-Lanesboro border.

At mile 3.4, pass under a powerline, and at mile 3.8, reach the junction with the side trail to the designated campsite at Crystal Mountain. Cross the brook and reach a hemlock grove with a view of the west side of Gore Pond at mile 4.2.

You may want to continue another .5 mile and hike around the shore of Gore Pond to its outlet where an old logging road provides access to the west side of the pond. This will add another mile to your hike and another half hour or so to your time.

To return to your vehicle, follow the A.T. south back to Gulf Road.

Trailhead Directions
Head east on Massachusetts 8/9 in Dalton, Massachusetts, and turn left onto Park Avenue. Follow Park Avenue for .5 mile to its junction with Gulf Road. The A.T. turns left onto Gulf Road.

WARNER HILL

EASY
1.8 miles roundtrip
1 hour

In the fall, after the leaves have fallen, there are some nice views from Warner Hill. This a pretty and leisurely day hike.

The Hike
From the paved Blotz Road, head south on the A.T. and climb .9 mile through a dense stand of evergreens to the top of Warner Hill. The summit of Warner Hill (elevation 2,050 feet) is marked by a cairn that sits a few feet to the left of the trail.
    Return north via the A.T.

Trailhead Directions
The A.T. crossing can be reached by following Blotz Road 6 miles east out of Pittsfield, Massachusetts, or for 1.3 miles west from Massachusetts 8.

FINERTY POND

MODERATE
4.8 miles roundtrip
4 hours

The highlights of this day hike are scenic Finerty Pond and the summits of Becket and Walling Mountains, which afford nice views. You will pass through parts of October Mountain State Forest (the largest in Massachusetts with more than 14,000 acres). This hike also features varied terrain.

The Hike
Beginning at the trail crossing on the paved Tyne Road, head north on the A.T., climbing toward the summit of Becket Mountain (elevation 2,180

feet), which you will reach in just over .5 mile. On the summit you will see concrete footings that mark the site of a former fire tower.

Continue along the ridge for another .75 mile toward Walling Mountain. You will have a nice view to the south of the hills around the large Goose Pond. At mile 1.6, reach the overgrown summit of Walling Mountain (elevation 2,220 feet).

From the summit, descend over a rocky trail for .5 mile to Finerty Pond, the destination of the hike. You can skirt the pond on stepping stones for .25 mile or so until the A.T. turns north away from the pond. If you hike further, you will add only half an hour or less to your time.

To return to Tyne Road, follow the A.T. south.

Trailhead Directions
Reach the A.T. crossing by following Tyne Road 3.5 miles east of Becket, Massachusetts, or .9 miles west of US 20.

Upper Goose Pond

MODERATE
4.8 miles roundtrip
4 hours

Purchased by the National Park Service for the A.T. Corridor, Upper Goose Pond is one of the more outstanding features along the A.T. in Massachusetts. Arriving at this pretty New England pond, you will discover the reason for its name—Upper Goose Pond is the nesting site and home of many Canada Geese.

The Hike
From the trail crossing on US 20 (Jacob's Ladder Highway), follow the trail south. In .25 mile, you will cross a stream on a high bridge. This is a historic mill site as well as an outlet of Greenwater Pond.

In another .1 mile, you will cross the Massachusetts Turnpike (Interstate 90) on twin bridges. Once off the bridge, you will enter the woods and make a steep ascent on rough trail, which eventually crosses two intermittent brooks.

At mile 1, reach the top of the ridge and a trail junction with a register box. Hike another .6 mile to the junction with the side trail to Upper Goose

Pond Cabin, which is .5 mile away. There is also a camping area at the Cabin, and a caretaker (in season) collects the fees for the cabin ($3) and the tent sites ($2).

Continue along the A.T. and pass an old chimney and a plaque marking the site of the old Mohhekennuck fishing and hunting club at mile 1.9. For the next .5 mile, the A.T. follows the shore of Upper Goose Pond before crossing its inlet at mile 2.4.

Follow the A.T. north back to US 20.

Trailhead Directions
The A.T. crossing at US 20 is 5 miles east of Exit 2 of the Massachusetts Turnpike (I-90). There is a parking area about .25 mile to the west of the trail crossing.

COBBLE HILL

EASY
4 miles roundtrip
2 hours

This gradual climb to the top of Cobble Hill offers fine views of the Tyringham Valley. Although there is a stile over a fence to cross and several bog bridges, this is an otherwise easy hike and a good choice for hiking with children and makes for a leisurely afternoon stroll along the A.T.

The Hike
From the trailhead on Main Road, follow the A.T. south. In .1 mile, cross Hop Brook on a footbridge. At mile .75, pass through a hemlock grove and cross a small stream. In another .25 mile, cross Jerusalem Road, which puts you in the Tyringham Cobble Reservation. Hike .25 mile from the road crossing to reach the .25-mile side trail to the top of Cobble Hill.

Return to the A.T. and follow it north to the trailhead on Main Road.

Trailhead Directions
The A.T. crosses Main Road 5 miles southeast (.9 mile past Tyringham) of US 20 at Lee, Massachusetts. Limited parking is available along the road.

BENEDICT POND AND THE LEDGES

MODERATE
3 miles roundtrip
2 hours

This hike has an unusual trailhead—a beach. From the swimming area on Benedict Pond, you will hike on a side trail along this beautiful glacial pond and then on the A.T. Your destination is The Ledges, a rocky ridge that affords fine views of Mount Everett and East Mountain. The Catskills can also be seen rising in the distance.

This hike is quite steep in some places but is only rated as moderate because it is relatively short in length. You may want to save time for a swim in the Pond. Canoes are also rented by the hour at the beach.

The Hike
From the swimming area on Benedict Pond, follow the Pond Loop Trail around the south side of the pond. At mile .5, reach the junction with the A.T. Turn left and follow the A.T. north. In .4 mile, cross the Benedict Pond outlet. The trail begins to ascend steeply for .6 mile as it climbs up to The Ledges.

To return, hike on the A.T. to the Pond Loop Trail, which you follow back to the trailhead.

Trailhead Directions
From US 23 in Monterey, Massachusetts, go north on Blue Hill Road for 2 miles to the entrance for the Beartown State Forest Entrance. Follow the signs to the swimming area at Benedict Pond.

EAST MOUNTAIN

MODERATE
2.8 miles roundtrip
2 hours

This short hike leads to East Mountain Ridge where you will find many overlooks. The views to the south and west of Mount Everett, the Housatonic River Valley, and the distant Catskills are well worth traversing this sometimes tricky trail. On the way to the ridge, this trail leads through glacial boulders.

The Hike
From Homes Road, follow the A.T. north and begin climbing, gradually at first and then more steeply. One mile from Homes Road, you will reach the high point on the ridge. The next .4 mile offers several fine views. The end of this hike is marked by a large boulder at mile 1.4. There is an outstanding view to the south.

Return to the trailhead by way of the A.T.

Trailhead Directions
From US 7, about 1.5 miles south of Great Barrington, Massachusetts, go east on Brush Hill Road, which becomes Homes Road. The A.T. crosses the road just over 2 miles from US 7. There is limited parking along the road.

Jug End

STRENUOUS
2.2 miles roundtrip
2 hours

This short, steep hike leads to tremendous views of the Housatonic River Valley, Mount Greylock and the rest of the Berkshires.

The Hike
From Jug End Road, follow the A.T. south and ascend gradually for .25 mile. The climb then becomes quite steep. At mile .75, there is a good view from an exposed rock face. In another .4 mile, you will reach the summit of Jug End.

To return, hike the A.T. back down to Jug End Road.

Trailhead Directions
From Massachusetts 41, 6 miles north of the Connecticut state line, turn left on Curtiss Road. This road becomes Jug End Road and reaches the trailhead in 1.5 miles. There is adequate parking at the trailhead.

JUG END AND MOUNT EVERETT

STRENUOUS
9.2 miles roundtrip
7 hours

This hike leads to tremendous views of the Housatonic River Valley, Mount Greylock and the rest of the Berkshires atop Jug End. The hike then continues on to the ninth highest peak in Massachusetts, Mount Everett, which has a panoramic view of the Taconic and Berkshire Ranges.

The Hike

From Jug End Road, follow the A.T. south and ascend gradually for .25 mile. The climb then becomes quite steep. At mile .75, there is a good view from an exposed rock face. In another .4 mile, reach the summit of Jug End.

Continue on the A.T., cross two unnamed peaks, and reach the summit of Mount Bushnell (elevation 1,834 feet) at mile 1.2. From Mount Bushnell, hike 1.1 miles to Glen Brook Shelter. In another .5 mile, reach the Guilder Pond Picnic Area. The pond is on your right. There is a loop trail around the pond, which uses the A.T. to complete the loop.

From the picnic area, hike .7 mile to the summit of Mount Everett (elevation 2,602 feet). The firetower is closed to the public, but you don't need to go to the top of it to enjoy the outstanding views from the summit.

Return via the A.T. back down to Jug End Road.

Trailhead Directions

From Massachusetts 41, 6 miles north of the Connecticut state line, turn left on Curtiss Road. This road becomes Jug End Road and reaches the trailhead in 1.5 miles. There is adequate parking at the trailhead.

MOUNT EVERETT

STRENUOUS
6.2 miles roundtrip
4 1/2 hours

The goal of this day hike is to reach the summit of Mount Everett, Massachusetts' ninth highest mountain, where you will have a commanding view of the Taconic and Berkshire Ranges, the Housatonic River Valley, and the distant Catskills. You will pass by a number of waterfalls on the Race Brook Trail as you make your way up to the A.T. The highest fall is nearly 100 feet tall.

The Hike
From the trailhead on Massachusetts 41, hike west on the blue-blazed Race Brook Falls Trail. In .25 mile, the gradual ascent will get steeper as you climb up out of the valley. At mile 1, there is a fine view of the Housatonic Valley, and at mile 2, reach a designated campsite with a privy and platforms for tents. In another .4 mile, reach the junction with the A.T. Turn right on the A.T. and begin climbing the south side of Mount Everett. After a .75-mile rocky and often steep climb, you will reach the open summit of Mount Everett.

Return via the Appalachian and Race Brook Falls Trails to the trailhead on Massachusetts 41.

Trailhead Directions
The parking lot for the Race Brook Trail is on Massachusetts 41, 3 miles north of the Connecticut state line at the junction of Massachusetts 41 and Salisbury Road, which leads east to Sheffield, Massachusetts.

CONNECTICUT

CONNECTICUT

From the state line of Massachusetts, the Appalachian Trail climbs up Bear Mountain as it enters Connecticut. The trail follows the Taconic Range to its southern end at Lions Head where there is an outstanding panoramic view. The A.T. then crosses a few mountains and follows along the Housatonic River. The A.T. traverses 52 miles in western Connecticut.

Alhough the mountains in Connecticut are all under 2,400 feet in elevation, there are many fine viewpoints in this section of the A.T. The highpoints—Lions Head, Rand's View, Hang Glider View and others—offer commanding views of the countryside.

Often referred to as the most photographed section of trail in the state, the red pine grove along the Houstaonic River north of Kent is dying a slow death. The trees, which are not native to the area, are being killed by a parasite and will all be dead within a few years. You should visit this special place while there is still time.

The A.T. crosses into and out of New York on the side of Schaghticoke Mountain and then crosses into New York a final time at Hoyt Road, 7 miles farther.

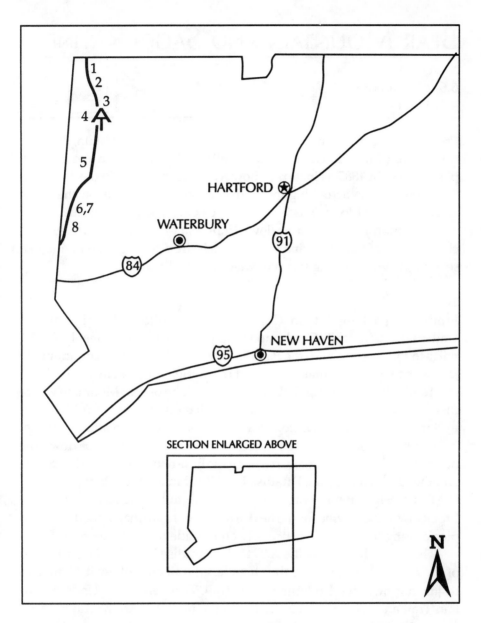

1. Bear Mountain and Sages Ravine
2. Lions Head
3. Rand's View
4. Mount Easter
5. Pine Knob
6. River Walk to Red Pine Plantation
7. St. John's Ledges to Caleb's Peak
8. Indian Rocks

BEAR MOUNTAIN AND SAGES RAVINE

MODERATE
6.6 mile roundtrip
4 1/2 hours

From the ruins of a stone tower on the summit of Bear Mountain, there are fine views of the Housatonic River Valley. The marker on the summit, placed there in 1885, is incorrect, however; this is not the highest point in Connecticut. The actual highpoint (elevation 2,380 feet) is on the south slope of nearby Mount Frissell, whose peak lies in Massachusetts.

The rough and rocky climb down from Bear Mountain leads to the cool, clear waters of Sages Ravine Brook, which drop through the ravine in a seemingly never ending series of waterfalls and pools.

The Hike
From the parking lot on Connecticut 41, follow the blue-blazed Undermountain Trail. Climb moderately and then more steeply for 1.1 miles to the junction with the Paradise Lane Trail. Turn left, continuing to follow the Undermountain Trail, and reach Riga Junction in .6 mile. Turn right and follow the A.T., climbing the south slope of Bear Mountain where there are many views along the climb. Reach the summit of Bear Mountain in .9 mile. The ruins of the stone tower offer a good observation platform.

Continue north on the A.T. Descend steeply over rock slabs down the north slope of Bear Mountain, reaching the base of the mountain in .25 mile and the junction with the Paradise Lane Trail in another .25 mile.

Reach Sages Ravine Brook in another .1 mile. The A.T. follows the Brook down the Ravine for the next .6 mile. There are many good places to picnic along the stream, particularly on the side opposite the trail.

The return hike is via the A.T. to the Paradise Lane Trail near the top of the ravine. Turn left onto the blue-blazed trail and follow it .75 mile to its junction with the Undermountain Trail. Turn left on the Undermountain Trail and follow it 1.6 miles down the mountain to the trailhead on Connecticut 41.

Trailhead Directions
The parking area on Connecticut 41 is about 4 miles north of US 44 in Salisbury, Connecticut.

LIONS HEAD

MODERATE
4.8 miles roundtrip
3 hours

The summit of Lions Head offers a magnificent 360-degree view of the surrounding countryside. The Twin Lakes can be seen far below to the east with Mount Prospect just to their south.

The Hike
From Connecticut 41, follow the A.T. north. In .25 mile, pass Plateau Campsite, which has a privy and tent sites. During a 1.5-mile moderate ascent, cross and recross an old road. The climb then can get steep at times. At mile 2.1, reach the junction with the Lions Head Trail. Continue following the A.T. and climb the last steep .25 mile to the summit of Lions Head. Hike .1 mile farther to the north summit of Lions Head where you will find views to the north of Bear Mountain, and beyond that, Mount Greylock in Massachusetts.

The return hike is via the A.T. to the parking lot on Connecticut 41.

Trailhead Directions
The parking lot on Connecticut 41 is located between two private residences, .75 mile north of US 44 in Salisbury, Connecticut.

RAND'S VIEW

MODERATE
6.8 miles roundtrip
3 1/2 hours

The A.T. in Connecticut offers many fine viewpoints, but the best of the best is Rand's View. This panoramic vista offers views of nearby Twin Lakes and Housatonic Valley, as well as the entire Taconic Range. Mount Greylock, Massachusett's highest peak, is 50 miles away, but it can be seen to the north on clear days.

If you would like a longer hike, Mount Prospect is .7 mile beyond Rand's View on the A.T.

The Hike

From the trailhead on US 44, follow the A.T. south, climbing Wetauwanchu Mountain (locally known as Barrack Matiff). Reach the high point of this mountain at mile .6 and a jeep road at mile 1.6. A buried cable right-of-way lies .25 mile past the jeep road. At mile 3.2, reach Billy's View, and in another .4 mile, reach Giant's Thumb, a noteworthy rock formation on the northern slope of Raccoon Hill.

The .1-mile side trail to Rand's View is .5 mile beyond the Giant's Thumb. If you would like to press on to the summit of Mount Prospect (elevation 1,461 feet), continue following the A.T. north for .75 mile. Mount Prospect offers fine views of the Housatonic River Valley.

The return hike, from either destination, is north on the A.T. to the trailhead on US 44.

Trailhead Directions

The parking area on US 44 is .5 mile north of Salisbury, Connecticut.

MOUNT EASTER

MODERATE
9.4 mile roundtrip
5 hours

There are several viewpoints along this hike, each a worthy destination—Belter's Bump, Hang Glider's View and Sharon Mountain.

The Hike

From the parking lot on US 7, hike south on the A.T. and follow an old roadbed to the Housatonic River. At mile .25, cross US 7 (no parking is available at this crossing) and cross fences on stiles. In .25 mile, reach Belter's Bump, a nice overlook. Continue following the A.T. south and reach Hang Glider's View 1.1 miles past the Bump.

For the next 2.1 miles, cross the northern and western slopes of Sharon Mountain (good views to the west) on the way to Mount Easter. Sharon Mountain is not a specific peak but an area with several views from the trail. At mile 4.7, reach the summit of Mount Easter, where there area also good views to the west.

The return hike is via the A.T. to the parking area on US 7.

Trailhead Directions
The parking lot on US 7 is about 1.5 miles south of Falls Village, Connecticut, and 5 miles north of West Cornwall, Connecticut.

PINE KNOB

MODERATE
3.2 miles roundtrip
2 1/2 hours

The highlights of this short day hike include several views of the Housatonic River Valley.

The Hike
From the trail crossing on Connecticut 4, follow the A.T. north and cross pretty Guinea Brook at mile .1. During periods of high water, you can avoid crossing the brook by remaining on Connecticut 4 until you see a dirt road to the left. This road joins the trail on the other side of the brook. Cross the dirt Sharon Road in another .1 mile. A blue-blazed side trail here (the old A.T.) leads .5 mile to the Pine Knob Loop Trailhead and a parking area on US 7.

At mile .5, reach a side trail that leads .1 mile to the summit of Breadloaf Mountain located on private property. At mile 1.4, cross Hatch Brook, and at mile 1.5, reach the junction with the Pine Knob Loop Trail. The Pine Knob Loop Trail heads right to US 7 and Housatonic Meadows State Campground. The two trails converge for .1 mile leading to Pine Knob and wonderful views of the Housatonic River Valley.

You can return to Connecticut 4 by following the A.T. south.

Trailhead Directions
The trail crossing at Connecticut 4 is 1 mile west of Cornwall Bridge.

River Walk to Red Pine Plantation

EASY
3.2 miles roundtrip
2 hours

This level section of trail ambles along the Housatonic River and contains several archaeological sites said to be more than 9,000 years old. The destination of this hike is a beautiful red pine plantation. Planted in the early 1930s, the red pines are a failed experiment. They are already dying of a blight and are also unable to survive the Connecticut climate. In spite of this, they did grow tall and are magnificent to behold—definitely worth a look before the blight kills them off.

The Hike
From St. John's Ledges on River Road, follow the A.T. north along the Housatonic River. In just over .5 mile, cross Mt. Brook, and .25 mile later, the site of the North Kent (Flanders) Bridge, destroyed by a flood in 1936.

This is the end of the town road, and from this point on (to the Sharon Town Line), the road has been legally abandoned and is off-limits to motor vehicles. Continue along the river and pass foundations in an old orchard in .5 mile and soon after reach the red pine plantation.

Return to the parking area by retracing your footsteps south along the A.T.

Trailhead Directions
The parking area below St. Johns Ledges is 3 miles north of Connecticut 341 in Kent. Take Connecticut 341 west and turn right on Skiff Mountain Road after crossing the Housatonic River. Follow this road for 1 mile, bearing right on River Road. Travel another 1.7 miles (the road turns to dirt before reaching the ledges) to the trailhead.

St. Johns Ledges and Caleb's Peak

MODERATE
2.2 miles roundtrip
1 hour

This hike has both a steep ascent and descent—up to and down from St. Johns Ledges—but the climb is less than .5 mile and you are aided by ninety rock steps installed by a trail crew from the Appalachian Mountain Club. The cliffs around the St. Johns Ledges are often used for rock climbing instruction. Both St. Johns Ledges and Caleb's Peak offer wonderful views.

The Hike
From River Road, enter the woods heading south on the A.T. The trail travels west toward the base of St. Johns Ledges, and soon reaches the ascent up ninety stone steps. At mile .6, reach the top of the ledges and good views of the Housatonic Valley and the town of Kent.

Continue south along the A.T. for another .5 mile to Caleb's Peak (elevation 1,160 feet). The ledge outcropping on its summit provides great views to the south.

Return north to the parking area on River Road via the A.T.

Trailhead Directions
The parking area below St. Johns Ledges is 3 miles north of Connecticut 341 in Kent. Take Connecticut 341 west and turn right on Skiff Mountain Road after crossing the Housatonic River. Follow this road for 1 mile, bearing right on River Road. Travel another 1.7 miles (the road turns to dirt before reaching the ledges) to the trailhead.

Indian Rocks

MODERATE
6.8 miles roundtrip
5 hours

This hike ascends Mount Algo and follows the ridge along Schaghticoke Mountain. At Indian Rocks, the trail is on the Schaghticoke Indian Reservation, which is part of the last major Indian stronghold in Connecticut. Indian settlements at the confluence of the Housatonic and Ten Mile Rivers date back to prehistory, and in 1730, more than 100 Indian families still lived in the area.

The Hike

From Connecticut 341, follow the A.T. south, ascending through the woods. At .1 mile, follow a woods road to the right for a short distance before heading left into the woods and ascending gradually.

At mile .25, a side trail leads right to water and the Mount Algo Lean-to. Continue along the A.T. and reach the height of the land at mile .9, and cross Thayer Brook at mile 1.2. After Thayer Brook, ascend steeply up a rocky path to the high point of Schaghticoke Mountain at mile 2. From here, the trail follows ledges that offer good views to the south.

In another .75 mile, descend into Rattlesnake Den, a ravine with large hemlocks and tumbled boulders. After crossing a brook, you will ascend gradually. There is water here as well as a campsite with a privy on a side trail.

In another .25 mile, descend into Dry Gulch, a rocky ravine, and climb out of it, steeply. From here, you will climb along the eastern slope of Schaghticoke and reach Indian Rocks at mile 3.4. This overlook has views to the east of the Housatonic River Valley.

From here, return north to Connecticut 341 via the A.T.

Trailhead Directions

From Kent, Connecticut, travel .75 mile west on Connecticut 341 to the trail crossing. There is parking .25 mile west of the crossing at the junction of Connecticut 341 and Schaghticoke Road.

NEW YORK

NEW YORK

The 92 miles of the Appalachian Trail in New York travels from Schaghti-coke Mountain on the Connecticut line to the Kittatinny Range in New Jersey, passing through Fahnestock and Harriman-Bear Mountain State Parks. Just south of the Bear Mountain Bridge, the A.T. reaches its lowest point at the Trailside Zoo in Bear Mountain Park (elevation 124 feet). Hikers are no longer charged a toll for walking across the bridge.

The trail immediately south of the Bear Mountain Bridge was the first section of the A.T. to be built. It was cleared in 1923 by a group from the New York-New Jersey Trail Conference. That group still maintains the trail in New York and New Jersey to this day.

New York City's skyline can be seen on a clear day from several points along the A.T. in New York, including West Mountain Shelter and Mombasha High Point. After passing through Harriman-Bear Mountain Parks, the A.T. travels west, then south, leaving New York near Prospect Rock.

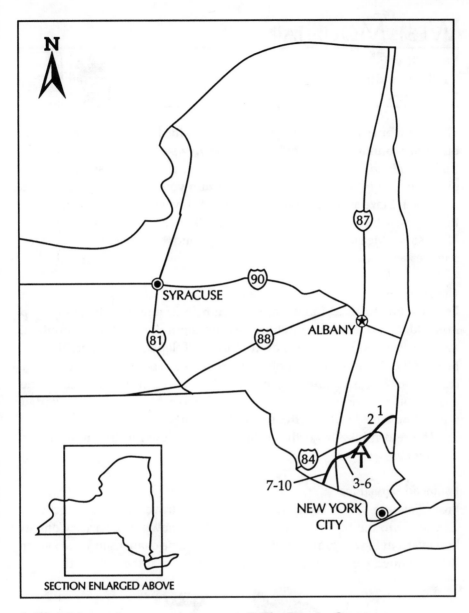

1. West Mountain
2. Mount Egbert
3. West Slope of Hosner Mountain
4. Shenandoah Mountain
5. Denning Hill
6. Denning Hill Traverse
7. The Lemon Squeezer
8. Buchanan Mountain
9. Fitzgerald Falls and Mombasha
   High Point
10. Prospect Rock

WEST MOUNTAIN

MODERATE
2 miles roundtrip
1 1/2 hours

This short, but sometimes steep climb leads to the highest of several peaks on West Mountain, which offers two fine views of the surrounding New York farmland. At the trailhead, a large oak tree, which stands on the opposite side of the road from the direction you will be hiking, bears a white A.T. blaze and is known locally as the Dover Oak. It is believed to be the largest white oak on the A.T. (though there are bigger white oaks in New York). Measured 4^1/$_2$ feet from the ground, the Dover Oak is 19 feet, 5 inches around.

The Hike

From County Road 20, follow the A.T. south. In .25 mile, pass through a gap in an old rock wall and begin climbing the eastern slope of West Mountain. At mile .7, pass the .1-mile side trail to the Telephone Pioneers Shelter. Beyond the shelter (.25 mile uphill), there is a short side trail to a nice view from a rock ledge. Continuing on the A.T., hike .1 mile south to reach the summit of West Mountain (elevation 1,225 feet), where you'll be rewarded with a fine view to the north of rural New York.

The return hike is north on the A.T. back down to the trailhead on County 20.

Trailhead Directions

From Pawling, New York (at New York 22), travel 2.4 miles north on County 20 to the trail crossing. County 20 is known as Charles Colman Boulevard in Pawling, and after .25 mile, the name changes to West Dover Road. Limited parking is available along the road at the trailhead.

Mount Egbert

MODERATE
3.2 miles roundtrip
1 1/2 hours

There are two good views of rural New York along this short hike to the summit of Mount Egbert.

The Hike
From the trailhead on Depot Hill Road, hike south on the A.T. and soon descend into a small ravine. At .25 mile, begin climbing, and at mile .4, reach a viewpoint on a rock outcrop. It is .25 mile frrom that first viewpoint to the short side trail that leads to the Morgan Stewart Memorial Shelter. At mile 1.4 (.1 mile beyond the shelter), reach the summit of Mount Egbert (elevation 1,329 feet), and at mile 1.6, reach a second viewpoint on a rock outcrop.

Return by hiking back north on the A.T. to the Depot Hill Road.

Trailhead Directions
To get to the trailhead, drive north from West Pawling, New York, on New York 55 for 1.5 miles, and turn left on New York 216. After .4 mile (near Poughquag), turn left again as you keep following New York 216. In another .6 mile, turn left onto Depot Hill Road and travel 1.7 miles to the trailhead. Depot Hill Road is unpaved at the trailhead. Adequate parking is available along the road.

West Slope of Hosner Mountain

EASY
3.2 miles roundtrip
2 hours

This day hike is unusual because the trail never climbs to the top of the mountain you are hiking on; nevertheless, there are several fine views of the Hudson River Valley from this sidehill trail. The views are somewhat improved in the fall when the leaves fall off the trees, but this is also nice in the summer. You will be using an old section of the A.T. (now blue-blazed) to make a loop of part of the hike.

The Hike
From Hosner Mountain Road, hike south on the A.T. and begin climbing. In .25 mile, reach the .4 mile side trail that leads to Bailey Spring Campsite. Continue following the A.T. and climb Hosner Mountain, passing through a hemlock grove on your way up the ridge. There is a fine view of the Hudson River Valley to the north and west. At mile .75, reach a blue-blazed trail (the old A.T. that you will return on later), and continue following the white-blazed A.T. for another .6 mile to reach the southern end of the blue-blazed trail.

Following the blue-blazed trail, which takes a lower route across the ridge, hike back to the A.T. and return to the trailhead on Hosner Mountain Road.

Trailhead Directions
Hosner Mountain Road is the first road on the Taconic State Parkway as you head north past Interstate 84. Turn right off the Parkway and travel about .5 mile to a fork. Turn right, cross under I-84, and drive .25 mile to the trail crossing. There is limited parking available along the road at the trailhead.

SHENANDOAH MOUNTAIN

MODERATE	
8.4 miles roundtrip	
5 hours	

From the southern end of Canopus Lake, the A.T. heads north into Clarence Fahnestock Memorial State Park and then on to the summit of Shenandoah Mountain. There are wonderful views of Canopus Lake from the trail as well as a good view east from the summit of Shenandoah Mountain.

The Hike
From the A.T. crossing at the southern end of Canopus Lake (New York 301), the footpath heads right into the woods and begins a gentle descent. In .25 mile, after a steep ascent, the trails turns right. A short distance later, you will find a trail register on a tree to the right.

After another .1 mile, the trail levels off and begins a gentle descent. Then (.5 mile later), you will cross a rocky stream and parallel the west shore of Lake Canopus. There are some views of the lake through the trees.

At mile 2, you will cross a small stream and begin a steep climb (.25 mile later). The .1-mile climb leads to an outstanding viewpoint of Canopus Lake at its northern end. In .1 mile, there is another viewpoint to the west, and a short distance later, a side trail heads to another western-facing viewpoint. You will soon begin a gradual then steep descent, crossing a small stream at mile 2.8.

At .25 mile, you will turn left and follow an old woods road bordered by stone walls, and in .1 mile, you will pass the ruins of an old building. A short distance later, you will cross a stream (intermittent) and continue following the stone wall.

At mile 3.8, you will leave the woods road (.75 mile after you joined it) and begin to ascend, reaching the open summit of Shenandoah Mountain (elevation 1,282 feet) at about mile 4.3. From the summit, there are beautiful views to the east and limited views to the west through the trees.

To return, follow the A.T. south back to New York 301 and the parking area.

Trailhead Directions
New York 301 and the trail crossing at the southern end of Canopus Lake are 1.5 miles southwest of the junction of New York 301 and the Taconic State Parkway. There is a parking area .25 mile east of the trail crossing on New York 301.

DENNING HILL

EASY
5 miles roundtrip
3 hours

This hike passes through an area rich in Revolutionary War history. The hills in the area, including Little Fort Hill, all bear names reminiscent of war days. The Old West Point Road once lead to Benedict Arnold's headquarters at Garrison. In this area on October 9, 1777, the British moved north from Peekskill to battle with the 2,000 Continentals camped at Continental Village, which is still a small town.

The high point of the hike, Denning Hill (elevation 900 feet), offers great views. On clear days, you may even see the skyline of New York City.

The Hike

The A.T. crosses the intersection of US 9 and New York 403 and heads north into the woods. After .25 mile, you will cross a swampy area on bog bridges and then the Old Highland Turnpike, a dirt road. The A.T. continues through the woods, turning left and following a cleared strip of land in another .25 mile.

At mile .5, following a brief but steep climb, you will pass through a grassy area and turn left onto a paved road. After crossing the paved Old West Point Road (the pavement ends here), you will continue downhill on a private gravel road, turning left off that road in .1 mile.

The trail enters the woods, passes through an overgrown field, and begins to climb Little Fort Hill. At mile 1.3, you will come to the junction of a side trail that heads right to Graymoor Monastery, and at mile 2, another side trail at the top of a rocky ascent leads to a viewpoint.

After .1 mile, you will turn right onto a woods road, and after another .1 mile, you will turn right again, leaving the woods road. (The woods road continues left a short distance to a good view of the Hudson River.) At mile 2.5, after a short but steep climb, you will reach the ridge of Denning Hill. After turning right, you will follow the ridge a short distance to a viewpoint in a clearing.

From here, follow the A.T. south back to US 9 and New York 403.

Trailhead Directions

The trail crossing at the junction of US 9 and New York 403 is 4 miles north of the US 9-US 6/202 intersection, which is just north of Peekskill, New York. Parking is available on a short road between US 9 and New York 403, about .1 mile from the trail crossing.

DENNING HILL TRAVERSE

EASY
5 mile traverse
3 hours

This is a hike that passes through an area rich in Revolutionary War history. The hills in the area, including Little Fort Hill, all bear names reminiscent of war days. The Old West Point Road once lead to Benedict Arnold's headquarters at Garrison. In this area on October 9, 1777, the British moved north from Peekskill to battle with the 2,000 Continentals camped at Continental Village, which is still a small town.

The high point of the hike, Denning Hill (elevation 900 feet), offers great views. On clear days, you may even see the skyline of New York City. Because this hike is a traverse, you will need a shuttle or someone to drop you off and pick you up. Because there is no parking on Canopus Hill Road, a vehicle cannot be left there.

The Hike

The A.T. crosses the intersection of US 9 and New York 403 and heads north into the woods. After .25 mile, you will cross a swampy area on bog bridges and then the Old Highland Turnpike, a dirt road. The A.T. continues through the woods, turning left and following a cleared strip of land in another .25 mile.

At mile .5, following a brief but steep climb, you will pass through a grassy area and turn left onto a paved road. After crossing the paved Old West Point Road (the pavement ends here), you will continue downhill on a private gravel road, turning left off that road in .1 mile.

The trail enters the woods, passes through an overgrown field, and begins to climb Little Fort Hill. At mile 1.3, you will come to the junction of a side trail that heads right to Graymoor Monastery, and at mile 2, another side trail at the top of a rocky ascent leads to a viewpoint.

After .1 mile, you will turn right onto a woods road, and after another .1 mile, you will turn right again, leaving the woods road. (The woods road continues left a short distance to a good view of the Hudson River.)

At mile 2.5, after a short but steep climb, you will reach the ridge of Denning Hill. After turning right, you will follow the ridge a short distance to a viewpoint in a clearing. From the viewpoint, continue along the stone wall a short distance before turning left and descending. At mile 2.7, you will descend steeply along a rocky area, and at mile 3, you will ascend steeply up a rocky area. The trail then continues along the side of the hill, descends, and crosses a swampy area on bog bridges.

A short distance later, you will reach Old Albany Post Road (dirt) and its intersection with Chapman Road. Cross the road diagonally to the left and enter the woods, crossing a wet area on rocks before climbing steeply.

After .1 mile, you will pass through a blueberry patch as the path levels off, and after another .25 mile, you will pass through a gap in a stone wall. At mile 4, cross several stone walls, and after the walls, turn right and climb steeply through mountain laurel.

At the top of Canopus Hill (mile 4.3), the trail levels off and there is a viewpoint in a cleared area a short distance later. From here, the trail turns left and descends steeply, and .25 mile later, you will pass a large hemlock tree to the right of the trail where the descent will become more moderate. At mile 4.9, you will cross a brook, and at mile 5, you will reach Canopus Hill Road (dirt), the end of this traverse.

Trailhead Directions

The trail crossing at the junction of US 9 and New York 403 is 4 miles north of the US 9-US 6/202 intersection, which is just north of Peekskill, New York. Parking is available on a short road between US 9 and New York 403, about .1 mile from the trail crossing. There is no parking on Canopus Hill Road so a traverse would require a shuttle. Canopus Hill Road, a dirt road, is .25 mile west of its intersection with Canopus Hollow Road at Canopus Valley Crossroads. It can also be reached by taking the Old Albany Post Road off US 9 near Nelson Corners to its intersection with Canopus Hill Road—about 2 miles. From there, it is just over 1 mile to the trail crossing.

THE LEMON SQUEEZER

EASY
6 miles roundtrip
3 hours

Lemon Squeezer, a narrow, steep passage between two boulders, is the highlight of this trip, but the area is rich in history as well. The Greenwood Ironworks in nearby Arden was built in 1811. The tens of thousands of tons of magnetite ore brought from this area was made into pig iron and then was shipped to a foundry at West Point to make guns and shells.

The iron industry hit its boom here during the Civil War, but when smelting with coal replaced smelting with charcoal, the industry moved south to Pennsylvania, and by the 1890s, was all but gone from Arden.

This area was also once inhabited by many Indian tribes, the last being the Algonquins, and thus the preponderance of Indian names—Ramapo, Tiorati, Tuxedo. Most of the bodies of water given Indian names are man-made, though, and have no relation to the tribes that once resided here.

Thanks to Daniel Chazin for checking out the 1994 relocation and rewriting some of this hike description to keep the book current as it goes to press. Because the relocation was not completed by press time, you will want to be particularly careful to follow the white blazes, even if the trail seems to differ from the description in this book.

The Hike

From the Elk Pen parking area, walk back to Arden Valley Road and follow the white A.T. blazes north. The A.T. here runs concurrently with the Arden-Surebridge Trail (A-SB), which is marked with a red triangle on white blazes.

After .1 mile, you will turn right onto a chained-off woods road (Old Arden Road) and skirt the Elk Pen Field to the right. The metal fence around this field is all that is left of the Park's early attempt to establish an elk herd here. The A-SB continues straight ahead on the paved road. The Old Arden Road once connected the Arden estate of financier and railroad magnate Edward R. Harriman with the town of Tuxedo, but the road was partially destroyed when the New York Thruway was built.

In about 500 feet, you will turn left into the woods and begin to climb. In about another .6 mile, you will reach the summit of Green Pond Mountain, with good views to the north. Then you will descend the eastern slope of the mountain.

At mile 1.4, you will reach a dirt road, Island Pond Road, and turn right. The Trail soon turns off the road and goes up a set of log steps. In another 250 feet, you will cross a gravel road which provides access for fishermen to Island Pond. Then you will descend and, in another 300 feet, cross a wooden bridge over the outlet of Island Pond. The outlet is partially channeled into a spillway made of cut stones. This spillway was constructed by the CCC in 1934, as a part of a plan to dam the pond, and thereby enlarge it. However, the work was never completed, and the pond remains in its natural state.

After crossing the bridge, you will climb to a viewpoint over Island Pond, and then descend. At mile 1.8, you will turn right onto the Crooked Road, an old woods road, and immediately cross the inlet of Island Pond. Follow the road for 300 feet, and then turn left into the woods. After climbing for some distance, you will descend briefly and, at mile 2, reach the Lemon Squeezer. The A-SB joins the A.T. again from the right, and both trails climb the 300 feet through the Lemon Squeezer, a narrow (and steep) passage between boulders.

Once through the boulders, return to the Elk Pen parking area by retracing your steps south on the A.T. Or, if you prefer, you can go back on the A-SB Trail. If you choose this alternative, continue straight ahead, following the joint A.T. and A-SB blazes. In .3 mile, you will reach the summit of Island Pond Mountain, the site of a former fire tower. Descend to a viewpoint over Island Pond, and continue descending more steeply over ledges, until you reach the paved Arden Valley Road in another .5 mile. The trail crosses the paved road, then crosses the outlet stream from Island Pond, and recrosses the road. Continue downhill for another .4 mile where the A-SB rejoins the Arden Valley Road, and follows it for .9 mile back to the Elk Pen parking area.

Trailhead Directions
The trail crosses New York 17 at its intersection with Arden Valley Road, .75 mile south of Arden. Parking is available at the Elk Pen parking area, .25 mile east of New York 17 on Arden Valley Road.

BUCHANAN MOUNTAIN

EASY
1.6 miles roundtrip
1 hour

Highlights of this short day hike include views from the first and second summits of Buchanan Mountain (elevation 1,142 feet).

The Hike
From the A.T. crossing at East Mombasha Road, enter the woods heading south and climb steadily. In .25 mile, you will reach the first viewpoint on the secondary summit of Buchanan Mountain. Enjoy views to the east over Little Dam Lake.

Descend steeply to a rocky, hemlock-covered slope and continue along the footpath. In .1 mile, cross a stream, and in another .1 mile, cross a second stream. At mile .5, you will cross the third stream in your descent before climbing the final .25 mile to the primary summit of Buchanan Mountain.

After enjoying the view, turn around and head back to the parking area on East Mombasha Road.

Trailhead Directions
The trail crossing at East Mombasha Road can be reached by taking the Orange Turnpike off New York 17 in Southfields, and bearing left on West Mombasha Road at the fork. Shortly thereafter, turn right onto East Mombasha Road and follow it less than .5 mile to the trail crossing. Only day parking is permitted at the trail crossing.

FITZGERALD FALLS AND MOMBASHA HIGH POINT

EASY
4.6 miles roundtrip
3 hours

This day hike will take you to the beautiful Fitzgerald Falls and Mombasha High Point, where there are good views. On especially clear days, New York City can be seen from the High Point.

The Hike

From the A.T. crossing at Lakes Road (Monroe Road), the footpath descends, and crosses a wood truss bridge over Trout Brook. In .25 mile, you will cross another brook; turn left and follow the brook through a hemlock grove. Because this area is frequently flooded, there is a blue-blazed bypass trail to avoid the crossing of two more brooks in wet weather. The side trail ascends to the right through hemlocks and rejoins the A.T. after .1 mile (at Fitzgerald Falls).

Fitzgerald Falls flows twenty-five feet through a rocky cleft. Crossing the stream just below the falls, you will climb steeply up rock steps alongside the falls. After .1 mile, you will cross a stream and a tributary stream before passing through a hemlock grove, and in another .1 mile, you will cross another tributary stream and a dirt road as you continue to ascend. At mile .75, you will pass some stone walls to the left. These are the remains of an abandoned settlement.

Just over .5 mile later, make a left turn before climbing steadily .1 mile later. At mile 1.5, at the top of a rise, the blue-blazed Allis Trail heads off to the right. A viewpoint is located a short distance north on the Allis Trail, which was named for an early treasurer of the Applachian Trail Conference. From the viewpoint, High Point Monument in New Jersey and Mount Tammany at the Pennsylvania/New Jersey border are visible to the west.

The trail levels off here and reaches Mombasha High Point (elevation 1,280 feet) in another .75 mile. To the left is Mombasha Lake with Shunemunk Mountain behind it to the northeast. Kloiber's Pond can be seen straight ahead along West Mombasha Road; Harriman State Park can be seen to the east. New York City can be seen on the horizon to the south on clear days, and Bellvale Mountain is to the west.

Return to the parking area on Lakes Road by heading south on the A.T.

Trailhead Directions
To reach the trail crossing, take Lakes (Monroe) Road out of Greenwood Lake, New York, and travel about 4 miles.

PROSPECT ROCK

EASY
3.4 miles roundtrip
2 hours

Prospect Rock, with its magnificent views of Greenwood Lake and the Taylor Mountains, is the destination of this hike. You will walk the State Line Trail to access the A.T.

The Hike
Beginning at the trailhead of the State Line Trail on New York 210 (opposite the Greenwood Lake Marina), hike 1.2 miles along the New York-New Jersey border to the A.T. The State Line Trail ascends for .25 mile before turning right (houses are still in view here). For the next .25 mile, the trail uses log steps to prevent erosion.

At mile .75, the Ernest Walter Trail (yellow blazes) heads off to the left. This trail makes a loop around Surprise Lake and West Pond. After .1 mile, the State Line Trail turns sharply to the left and then to the right. For the next .4 mile, the trail heads west, crossing over the ridge of Bellvale Mountain with several short ascents and descents.

At mile 1.2, the State Line Trail joins the A.T. at the New York-New Jersey State Line, heading north on the A.T. for .1 mile to good western views from open rocks. After .25 mile, there is a trail register on a pine tree to the right of the trail, and .5 mile after joining the A.T. (following a short climb), you will reach Prospect Rock (elevation 1,433 feet).

Return by following the A.T. south for .5 mile, pick up the State Line Trail, and descend to Greenwood Lake.

Trailhead Directions
The State Line Trail begins opposite the Greenwood Lake Marina off of New York 210 in Greenwood Lake, New York.

NEW JERSEY

New Jersey

The New York/New Jersey state line runs along the ridge of Bearfort Mountain above Greenwood Lake. Passing through the Abram S. Hewitt State Forest, the first of New Jersey's 63 miles travel parallel to the New York/New Jersey state line. The trail passes through Wawayanda State Park before descending to Vernon, New Jersey.

Crossing the Vernon Valley, a former glacial lake, the trail soon ascends Pochuck Mountain and then descends to the Kittatinny Valley. The A.T. continues across the Kittatinny Valley to High Point State Park after passing Unionville, New York. This section of the trail is characterized by rolling farmland, pastures, fields and open woods.

High Point is, as the name implies, the highest point in the state of New Jersey. Although the A.T. does not actually reach the summit, there is a short side trail. From High Point State Park, the A.T. follows Kittatinny Ridge to Stokes State Forest, moving along a rocky footpath through hickory and scrub oak forests.

From Stokes State Forest, the trail continues along Kittatinny Ridge to Delaware Water Gap. It passes through Delaware Water Gap National Recreation Area and Worthington State Forest. The highlight of the southern end of the A.T. in New Jersey is Sunfish Pond, a beautiful glacial pool.

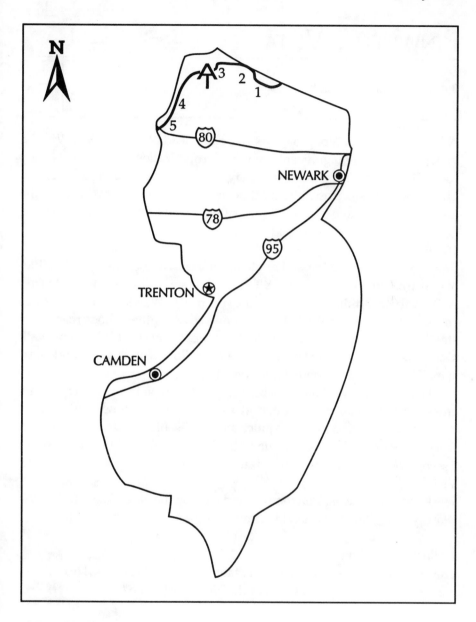

1. Pinwheel's Vista
2. Pochuck Mountain
3. High Point Monument
4. Rattlesnake Mountain
5. Sunfish Pond

Pinwheel's Vista

EASY
9.4 miles roundtrip
5 hours

A nice stroll, often along old woods roads, leads to Pinwheel's Vista, a viewpoint with a magnificent view of Vernon Valley and the Kittatinny Ridge. New York's Catskills and Shawangunks can be seen to the north. There are a few steep ascents and descents. Wawayanda was the name the Lenape Indians gave to a creek they called "water on the mountain."

The Hike
From the Wawayanda State Park headquarters, follow the .25-mile blue-blazed trail which leads to the A.T. Turn left and follow the white-blazed A.T. south. In .1 mile, reach the .1-mile side trail to Wawayanda Shelter and continue hiking along the A.T. as it follows several other woods roads. The steel bridge over a stream is 1.1 miles from the shelter side trail. As you walk along the mountain, the trail continues to follow woods roads and occasionally re-enter the woods for sections.

Two miles beyond the steel bridge, walk alongside a stream and then cross another stream near a waterfall. In .5 mile, cross a stone wall, descend and climb again, and reach the junction with the blue-blazed Wawayanda Ridge Trail at mile 4.5. Continue following the A.T. and in .1 mile, reach a second blue-blazed trail, which leads to the right for .1 mile to Pinwheel's Vista.

To return, hike back on the A.T. and pick up the blue-blazed trail to the Wawayanda State Park headquarters.

Trailhead Directions
The headquarters for Wawayanda State Park is on Warwick Turnpike in New Jersey about 3 miles south of the New York state line.

POCHUCK MOUNTAIN

MODERATE
3.8 miles roundtrip
2 1/2 hours

You will pass through some swampy areas on bog bridges on the way to Pochuck Mountain, which divides the Vernon and Kittatinny Valleys. A moderate climb leads to the wooded summit, which affords a pleasant view of the New Jersey farmland below.

The Hike
From County 565, hike south on the A.T., and cross a stream on a bridge in .1 mile, and begin climbing the southeastern slope of Pochuck Mountain. Cross an open field, and at mile .4, cross a wet area on bog bridges, then a small stream. In another .25 mile, cross a dirt road. From the road, hike .6 mile to the summit of Pochuck Mountain (elevation 1,130 feet). On the summit, a short side trail leads to a viewpoint where you'll find limited views of the valley below.
 Return on the A.T. to the trailhead on County 565.

Trailhead Directions
To reach the trailhead on paved County 565, travel about .4 mile south of the New York state line or about 1.3 miles north from Glenwood Lake.

HIGH POINT MONUMENT

MODERATE
2.8 miles roundtrip
2 hours

A moderate climb, with only one short, steep section, will take you to the highest point in the state. From both the wooden observation platform on the A.T. and from High Point Monument, you will be treated to a magnificent 360-degree view into three states—New Jersey, New York and Pennsylvania.

The Hike
From the parking lot at the park headquarters, follow the A.T. north, cross

New Jersey 23 and a grassy area along the road, and re-enter the woods. In .75 mile, there is a short, steep ascent. In another .25 mile, you will reach the observation tower with its commanding view of the area. From the platform, hike .25 mile to the blue-blazed side trail, which leads to High Point Monument. Follow the side trail for .25 mile to the summit (elevation 1,803 feet). To the west is Lake Marcia, which is just below the mountain in the park; in the distance, the Pocono Mountains in Pennsylvania; the southwest, Delaware Water Gap; and the east, the Kittatinny Valley and Pochuck and Wawayanda Mountains.

To return, hike on the blue-blazed trail, pick up the A.T., and head south to the parking lot at the park headquarters.

Trailhead Directions
To reach the headquarters for High Point State Park, follow US 6 east to New Jersey 23. The park headquarters is on New Jersey 23 about 7 miles south of Port Jervis, New York. Turn right into the parking lot, which the A.T. passes, and look for the trail crossing on the driveway near the road.

RATTLESNAKE MOUNTAIN

MODERATE
9.6 miles roundtrip
5 1/2 hours

A pleasant walk over gravel roads and trail takes you to the rocky summit of Rattlesnake Mountain. From the summit, overlooking the Poconos in Pennsylvania, there is a fine but limited view of the valley below.

The Hike
From Flatbrookville Road, which the A.T. follows for about 30 yards, hike north on the A.T. and cross a dirt road in .25 miles. In another 1.4 miles, cross a gravel road and descend a short, steep section before reaching a second gravel road at mile 1.8. A short blue-blazed side trail leads from this gravel road to a nice view of Crater Lake. Hike along gravel roads for the next 1.4 miles. At mile 3, a steep, 1.5-mile side trail leads to the base of Buttermilk Falls, which are 1,000 feet lower in elevation.

Continuing on the A.T., you will leave the gravel roads behind in .25 mile. In .75 mile, a short side trail leads to a viewpoint, and in .5 mile, after

a stream crossing, a blue-blazed side trail leads to water. Begin climbing for
.25 mile and reach the rocky summit of Rattlesnake Mountain (elevation
1,492 feet) where you'll find views to the west.

Return on the A.T. to the trailhead on Flatbrookville Road.

Trailhead Directions
The A.T. crosses Flatbrookville Road just over 3.2 miles east of Flatbrookville,
New Jersey. Parking is available along the side of the road about 50 yards
beyond the trail crossing.

SUNFISH POND

MODERATE
8.2 miles roundtrip
5 hours

This hike starts alongside Dunnfield Creek in Delaware Water Gap and
climbs Kittatinny Mountain to reach the cool, clear waters of Sunfish pond
(elevation 1,382 feet). The pond is a glacial lake high on the mountain.
Because this section is a favorite with day hikers, the area can get crowded
in the summer. If you want to avoid the crowds, try hiking during the week
if possible, or early in the day. By starting at the parking lot before 9 a.m.,
you may find some solitude at the pond.

The Hike
From the parking lot of the Dunnfield Creek Natural Area, hike north on
the A.T. and cross a bridge over Dunnfield Creek. In .4 mile, reach the
junction with a blue-blazed trail leading to Mount Tammany where you'll
find a spectacular view of Delaware Water Gap. Continuing north on the
A.T., hike 1.1 miles to reach the junction with the yellow-blazed Beulahland
Trail, and another 1.6 miles to the junction with the blue-blazed Douglas
Trail. Reach the southwest corner of the pond in .6 mile (mile 3.7).

The A.T. follows the edge of the pond for the next .75 mile. The return
hike is south on the A.T. to the parking lot at the trailhead.

Trailhead Directions
The parking lot of the Dunnfield Creek Natural Area is located in Delaware
Water Gap National Recreation Area. The recreation area is the first exit

after crossing the Interstate 80 toll bridge in Delaware Water Gap. For hikers coming down I-80 from New Jersey, the exit is the rest area just before the toll bridge. You will see the white-blazed A.T. as you pass by the information center. Follow the blazes as you drive to the parking lot at the trailhead, which is .5 mile beyond the information center.

PENNSYLVANIA

PENNSYLVANIA

With more than 230 miles to traverse, the Appalachian Trail in Pennsylvania is both one of the easiest and hardest to hike. The trail is often characterized by a tough climb up a ridge followed by a level but rocky walk.

The Appalachian Trail in Pennsylvania begins at Delaware Water Gap in the Kittatinny Mountains where it climbs more than 1,000 feet to the summit of Mount Minsi. This rough and rocky trail traverses the ridge from gap to gap (Totts, Fox, Wind, Smith, Little and finally the rocky face of Lehigh Gap).

For the next 30 miles (after you climb out of Lehigh Gap), the trail once again follows the ridge passing Bake Oven Knob, The Cliffs and Blue Mountain Summit before reaching the area of Hawk Mountain Sanctuary near Eckville. From here, the trail climbs once again to the ridge, passing The Pinnacle, an outstanding viewpoint over the Pennsylvania countryside.

From The Pinnacle, the A.T. drops down to Windsor Furnace, the site of an old iron stove plant; glassy slag can still be seen along the trail. The A.T. continues to Port Clinton where it regains the ridge and follows it for more than 30 miles. From Swatara Gap, the trail leaves Blue Mountain, crosses St. Anthony's Wilderness, and passes the sites of Rausch Gap and Yellow Gap Villages. After ascending Second Mountain, Sharp Mountain and Stony Mountain, the trail climbs to the ridge of Peters Mountain and follows it for 15 miles before descending to the Susquehanna River at Duncannon, Pennsylvania.

The A.T. heads southwest at the Susquehanna, crossing Cove and Blue Mountains and falling to the Cumberland Valley. This area was once famous for its road walk, but the trail has now been rerouted off roads through woods and rolling farmland. At the end of the valley, the trail climbs South Mountain, which it follows all the way through Maryland.

The southern section of trail in Pennsylvania passes through Boiling Springs with its beautiful Childrens Lake, Pine Grove Furnace State Park with its model furnace and Ironmasters Mansion, and Caledonia State Park with the Thaddeus Stevens Museum before it reaches the Pennsylvania/Maryland state line.

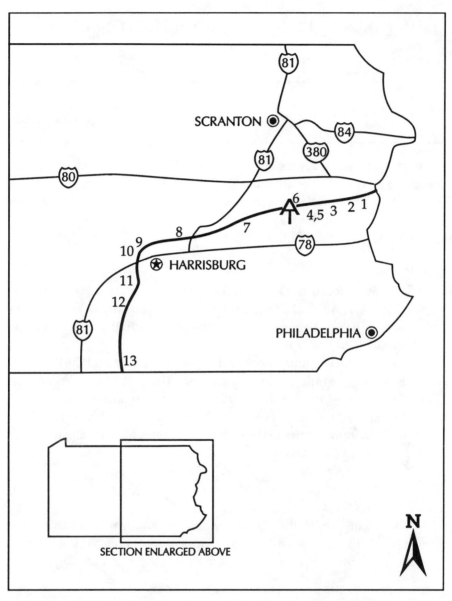

SECTION ENLARGED ABOVE

N

1. Winona Cliff, Lookout Rock, and Mt. Minsi
2. Wolf Rocks
3. Lookout Rock & Hahn's Lookout
4. Bake Oven Knob
5. Bear Rocks
6. The Cliffs and Bear Rocks
7. Windsor Furnace & Pinnacles
8. Rausch Gap Shelter
9. Table Rock
10. Hawk Rock
11. Boiling Springs
12. White Rocks Ridge
13. Chimney Rocks

Winona Cliff, Lookout Rock and Mount Minsi

MODERATE
4.6 miles roundtrip
5 hours

There are a few steep climbs on this hike, but the trail has much to offer. As you climb up from Delaware Water Gap, you will pass several outstanding views of Delaware Water Gap with Mount Tammany rising over the Delaware River. On the way to Mount Minsi, there are good views from Council Rock, Winona Cliff, and Lookout Rock.

The Hike
From Mountain Road in Delaware Water Gap (elevation 300 feet), hike south on the A.T. As you hike down a paved road, pass by Lake Lenape on the right at mile .1. Beyond the lake, the trail gradually climbs a ridge, which parallels the river below.

At mile .9, reach Council Rock and a view of the Gap and the Delaware River. In another .6 mile, reach Winona Cliff. This is the best viewpoint of Chief Tammany—look for the profile in the mountain across the river. Cross a stream in .1 mile, and reach Lookout Rock in another .1 mile. From Lookout Rock, hike .9 mile to the summit of Mount Minsi (elevation 1,461 feet), which is crossed on a gravel road.

The return hike is north on the A.T. to the trailhead.

Trailhead Directions
There is parking along the trail on Mountain Road, which turns off of Pennsylvania 611 in Delaware Water Gap, Pennsylvania. At the intersection, there is a prominent highway sign noting the A.T. crossing.

WOLF ROCKS

MODERATE
3.2 miles roundtrip
2 hours

The A.T. in Pennsylvania is said to be where old boots go to die because the rocky trail is so tough on boots (and feet). Wolf Rocks, which offers a nice view of Cherry Valley below, is one of the rockiest spots on the A.T. in this state. However, this hike to Wolf Rocks is easy; the worst of the rocks are west of the section you will be hiking. Be careful following the blazes at Wolf Rocks. If you wander off the trail, all of the rocks start to look alike and it can be difficult to find the trail again.

The Hike
From Pennsylvania 191 in Fox Gap, hike south on the A.T. and cross under a telephone line in .25 mile. Hike another .5 mile to where the trail joins a woods road and follow it for .6 mile. After leaving the woods road, hike .25 mile to Wolf Rocks.

The return hike is back down the A.T. to Fox Gap on Pennsylvania 191.

Trailhead Directions
There is a small parking area in Fox Gap about 4 miles south of Pennsylvania 611 on Pennsylvania 191.

LOOKOUT ROCK AND HAHN'S LOOKOUT

MODERATE
2 miles roundtrip
1 1/2 hours

It is a short, sometimes steep, climb up out of Wind Gap to Lookout Rock and Hahn's Lookout. These two viewpoints offer fine views of the Gap and the Poconos.

The Hike
From the parking lot in Wind Gap, follow the A.T. south along the road, cross under Pennsylvania 33, and follow the trail as it turns left and begins

climbing. It is a .75-mile ascent along switchbacks to Lookout Rock, where you will find views to the north. From Lookout Rock, climb another .25 mile to Hahn's Lookout, where you will find a view to the south of the town of Wind Gap and beyond.

The return hike is back down the A.T. to the trailhead.

Trailhead Directions
There is an entrance ramp onto Pennsylvania 33 in Wind Gap but no exit. To get to the trailhead, take Pennsylvania 33 to the town of Wind Gap. Take the main road north out of Wind Gap, and look for a well-marked dirt parking area about a mile beyond the center of town.

BAKE OVEN KNOB

EASY
.8 mile roundtrip
1/2 hour

This hike is really just a leg-stretcher. The goal is a magnificent view of the Pennsylvania farmland from Bake Oven Knob. This area is also a popular spot for hawk watching during the fall migrations.

The Hike
From Bake Oven Knob Road, hike north on the A.T. and reach the summit of Bake Oven Knob (elevation 1,560) at mile .4. There are a couple of vantage points—the first offers a view to the north, the second to the south.

Return to the parking lot by hiking south on the A.T.

Trailhead Directions
From Pennsylvania 895 in Andreas, Pennsylvania, Bake Oven Knob Road leads up to the Pennsylvania Game Commission parking lot near Bake Oven Knob.

BEAR ROCKS

EASY
2.8 miles roundtrip
2 1/2 hours

The highlights of this day hike include a magnificent 360-degree view of the Pennsylvania farmland from Bear Rocks.

The Hike
From Bake Oven Knob Road, hike south on the A.T. and reach a fork in the road at mile .4.

Turn left at the fork and reach Bear Rocks (elevation 1,664) at mile 1.4. There is a commanding view of the Pennsylvania farmland below.

Return on the A.T. north to the parking lot at Bake Oven Knob Road.

Trailhead Directions
From Pennsylvania 895 in Andreas, Pennsylvania, Bake Oven Knob Road leads up to the Pennsylvania Game Commission parking lot near Bake Oven Knob.

THE CLIFFS AND BEAR ROCKS

MODERATE
7 miles roundtrip
4 hours

This hike travels through one of the most scenic sections of the A.T. in Pennsylvania. The trail features a knife-edge walk along The Cliffs and panoramic views from Bear Rocks.

The Hike
From the restaurant on Pennsylvania 309, hike north along the A.T., which in this case means heading south along Pennsylvania 309 over the crest of Blue Mountain (elevation 1,360 feet). At mile .1, turn left off the road onto an eroded path, and a short distance later, turn right and then head left again.

At mile 1, reach the ridge and hike along an old woods road. Hike another .75 mile to a powerline cut-through and beyond to a rocky footpath and reach the junction with a blue-blazed trail that heads left .25 mile to the base of the valley and a short distance further to New Tripoli campsite and spring.

Continue along the A.T., turn left at mile 2.6, and follow the rocky knife edge known as The Cliffs, and look ahead to Bear Rocks. Reach the side trail to Bear Rocks at mile 3.5. It is a short hike along the blue-blazed side trail to the 360-degree views overlooking the Pennsylvania countryside.

From here, return south to Pennsylvania 309 via the A.T.

Trailhead Directions
The trail crossing at Blue Mountain Summit can be reached by traveling south from Snyders, Pennsylvania, on Pennsylvania 309. Parking is available in a game commission parking lot just north of the A.T. A sign marks the summit.

WINDSOR FURNACE, PULPIT ROCK AND THE PINNACLES

MODERATE
9.4 miles roundtrip
5 hours

From the site of Windsor Furnace, an early pig iron works, to the wonderful views from Pulpit Rock and The Pinnacles, this hike is full of interesting sights. Keep an eye out for the glassy slag in the footpath in the vicinity of Windsor Furnace. You can also see the remains of the old engine foundation in the undergrowth. Iron stoves were once manufactured here, and more interestingly, an iron replica of The Last Supper. Also, be on the lookout for charcoal hearths, which were used to fuel the furnace. These flat, round burning sites are thirty to fifty feet in diameter.

Pulpit Rock (elevation 1,582 feet) offers excellent views of The Pinnacle to the left and Blue Rocks in the foreground. Blue Rocks, a 40,000-year-old stretch of tumbled boulders left by the last glacial period, are more than a block wide and a mile long. They get their name from the quartzite and other minerals that give them their bluish hue early in the morning and on moonlit evenings. The tumbled rocks at The Pinnacles (elevation 1,635 feet) offer outstanding views of Pennsylvania farmland.

The Hike
From the parking area, hike north along the dirt road until you reach the A.T. crossing. Turn right onto the trail at the site of Windsor Furnace, follow a dirt road as it crosses Furnace Creek, and head right along a woods road.

Turn right again in .25 mile at the junction with a blue-blazed side trail that heads left a short distance to the Windsor Furnace Shelter. The water source is a questionable creek. From here, the A.T. ascends Blue Mountain, first moderately and then a bit more steeply.

At mile 2.5, pass the Astronomical Park of the Lehigh Valley Amateur Astronomical Society, and reach Pulpit Rock in .1 mile. There are views of The Pinnacles to the left and Blue Rocks in the foreground.

Continue along the A.T., pass a tower to your left in .1 mile, and an excellent view from a rock outcropping in another .1 mile. Pass a rock field to your left with good views to the north in .25 mile, pass through a cleft in a rock formation in another .1 mile, and soon thereafter pass through another rock field. Reach a yellow-blazed side trail at mile 4.3. The side trail heads downhill for 1.3 miles to Blue Rocks, and .25 mile beyond to Blue Rocks Campground (privately owned).

From the side trail, hike less than .5 mile to the blue-blazed side trail leading to The Pinnacles, which is a short distance off the A.T. Below The Pinnacles, there are a couple of caves and some sheer cliffs to explore, but watch out for copperheads.

From here, return to the parking area by retracing your footsteps south along the A.T.

Trailhead Directions
From Interstate 78/US 22, take Exit 9, Pennsylvania 61 South. From Pennsylvania 61 South, take the four-lane highway that heads east to Hamburg toward Lenhartsville. Nearly 3 miles after you turn on the four-lane highway, you will pass St. Pauls Church. Take the paved road on the left that becomes a dirt road in about .6 mile, about .4 mile after it passes under I-78. It is another .4 mile to the parking area and from there about .4 mile hike to the A.T. crossing.

RAUSCH GAP SHELTER

MODERATE
7.4 miles roundtrip
4 hours

This hike gives you the opportunity to explore Rausch Gap Village, an old coal mining community. If you wander through the area, you will turn up building foundations, a cemetery, hand-dug wells, abandoned railroad beds and railroad facilities of the Reading Railroad, and other remains of what was once a thriving industrial community. The village flourished in the 1850s and was large enough, at one point, to support a Catholic Mission. The three remaining markers in the cemetery are all members of the John Proud family and date from 1853.

The Hike

From the small parking lot on Pennsylvania 443, turn left (south) on the A.T. Hike about .5 mile and pass a road to the right. After another .25 mile, pass a grocery store on your right. At mile 1, turn right onto a macadam road.

At mile 1.4, head right onto a dirt road that passes through a housing development. Stay on the trail (road), and cross a stream with a dam to the right in .1 mile. Hike another .1 mile and turn left onto a dirt road between two houses. A blue-blazed trail to the right leads a short distance to the BleuBlaze Hostel.

Continue along the A.T., enter Pennsylvania Game Lands in .25 mile, and pass a woods road on your left in another .25 mile. Soon thereafter, turn left and ascend uphill. Except during the driest weather, there will be a spring in this section alongside the trail.

Reach the crest of Second Mountain in .5 mile, turn left, and descend along an old wagon road. After crossing Haystack Creek on a wooden footbridge at mile 3.5, hike .25 mile to the center of old Rausch Gap Village. The community well was to the left of the square. Take some time to explore the area and find the old cemetery, building foundations and more.

Return to the parking area by taking the A.T. north.

NOTE: A new state park is in the process of being constructed in the Swatara Gap area. During the construction of the dam and new highways, the trail will more than likely have to be relocated temporarily. Keep an eye out for new blazes.

Trailhead Directions
Take Exit 29 off Interstate 78/Interstate 81 toward Fort Indiantown Gap and National Cemetery. Follow Pennsylvania 443 north to the town of Green Point. The small parking area is .75 mile north of Larry's Green Point Country Store where the A.T. leaves the road for an open field.

TABLE ROCK

EASY
4.2 miles roundtrip
2 hours

Great views from Table Rock are the highlight of this day hike. A powerline cut-through along the way offers good views of the Susquehanna River, the longest river the A.T. crosses—444 miles.

The Hike
From the trailhead parking area, follow the A.T. north. Pass a radio facility of the Pennsylvania Fish Commission on your right in .25 mile, and cross a powerline cut-through in .5 mile with excellent views to the east of the Susquehanna River and Valley. Reach Zeager Shelter at mile 1.6. There are good views to the south from the shelter but no water. At mile 2, you will pass over Fumitory Rocks, and reach the junction with the short side trail to Table Rock Outlook .25 mile later. The side trail heads right to the outcropping. Bring a picnic lunch and enjoy the view. Return to the parking area by retracing your footsteps south along the A.T.

Trailhead Directions
The trailhead parking area is off Pennsylvania 225 on a dirt road at the crest of Peters Mountain. Travel north from the town of Dauphin at US 22/322 or south of Powells Valley. The A.T. follows the dirt road through the parking area.

HAWK ROCK

STRENUOUS
3 miles roundtrip
2 hours

This steep and strenuous climb leads to outstanding views from Hawk Rock, which overlooks the Susquehanna and Juniata Rivers and their valleys. There are also good views of Peters Mountain.

The Hike
After crossing the Shermans Creek Bridge in Duncannon, find a parking space. The A.T. follows this paved road for .25 mile after crossing the bridge—park anywhere in this area and follow the A.T. along the road.

In front of the old motel and bar, the trail turns sharply right and ascends steeply up Cove Mountain for .5 mile to an old mountain road. Climb the road along the north side of the ridge, and cross a rock slide at mile 1.2. The trail becomes a footpath again and reaches Hawk Rock at mile 1.5.

From here, return to Duncannon by following the A.T. north.

Trailhead Directions
From Market Street in Duncannon, pass underneath US 11/15. At the junction of Pennsylvania 274, turn left onto the old highway and follow it over the Shermans Creek Bridge.

BOILING SPRINGS

EASY
.6 mile roundtrip
1/2 hour

This short hike is centered around Children's Lake in Boiling Springs, Pennsylvania. The town is an eighteenth century community established around the iron industry and later became (nineteenth century) a vacation spot and recreation area. Today, listed on the National Register of Historic Places, Boiling Springs is mostly residential. The springs that fill Children's Lake are the highlight of this hike (although a stroll would probably be a more accurate description). More than 24,000 gallons bubble up through the ground each day. Parts of the lake are crystal clear, and ducks and geese add to the bucolic setting. The trail also passes a township park with a restored iron furnace.

The Hike
The hike begins at the Appalachian Trail Conference's Mid-Atlantic Headquarters in Boiling Springs. Following the blazes from the parking area, the trail leads you around Children's Lake, past a township park with a restored iron furnace, and to a stone arch highway bridge over Yellow Britches Creek.

Take some time to explore the area, especially some of the springs to the right of the conference headquarters. Bring a picnic lunch and enjoy the scenery.

Trailhead Directions
Limited parking is available at the ATC regional headquarters off Pennsylvania 174 in Boiling Springs.

WHITE ROCKS RIDGE

MODERATE
6.6 miles roundtrip
3 1/2 hours

White Rocks Ridge marks the northern end of the Blue Ridge Mountains, which begin in North Georgia. This pretty hike along a rocky ridge leads to the side trail to White Rocks Ridge, outcroppings of ancient quartzite dating back 550 million years. This ridge forms one of the outlines of greater South Mountain. The side trail is reached at Center Point Knob, which was once the mid-point of the A.T.

The Hike
Turning right into the woods at Whiskey Spring on Whiskey Spring Road, climb up Little Rocky Ridge. At mile .8, you will pass a rock outcropping on your right before descending off the ridge through woods.

At mile 1.3, cross a pipeline that looks like a narrow road, climb Murphy (Cabin) Hill, and descend to a charcoal hearth. From the hearth, hike another .9 mile to Little Dogwood Run. Immediately after crossing the run, reach the junction with an orange-blazed trail that leads 1.7 miles to Camp Tuckahoe, which belongs to the Boy Scouts of America. Shortly thereafter, reach the junction with a blue-blazed side trail that leads to the Alec Kennedy Shelter a short distance off the A.T.

After the side trail, ascend and descend along the side of Colon Hill and cross a woods road in 1 mile. Hike another .1 mile to Center Point Knob and reach the junction with the side trail to White Rocks Ridge. The side trail leads 1.2 miles to Kuhn Road. Follow the side trail as far as you wish, but you must return to the A.T. and retrace your footsteps back to Whiskey Spring Road to end the hike. In wet weather, the White Rocks Ridge side trail is wet and slippery, so you may wish to end your hike at Center Point Knob.

Trailhead Directions
From Pennsylvania 34 in Mount Holly Springs, turn right onto Mill Street (left if you are coming from Carlisle, 7 miles north). Follow Mill Street 2.3 miles to its junction with Petersburg Road. From here, travel 2.8 miles to the A.T. crossing. Petersburg Road becomes Whiskey Spring Road. Limited parking is available on the side of the road.

Chimney Rocks

STRENUOUS
2.6 miles roundtrip
2 hours

Chimney Rocks (elevation 1,940 feet) is the destination of this short but strenuous hike. There are outstanding views of Greenridge and the Waynesboro Reservoir from this magnificent outcropping.

The Hike
From the trail crossing at Antietam (Old Forge) Road, cross Tumbling Run on a bridge. The trail turns right off the road in .1 mile and begins to climb moderately, then steeply.

Reach the junction with the blue-blazed trail that leads a short distance to Tumbling Run Shelter and continues another .5 mile to Hermitage Cabin, which is run by the Potomac Appalachian Trail Club (PATC). The cabin is locked and reservations must be made to rent it. From Hermitage Cabin, the blue-blazed trail joins the A.T. in another .9 mile.

Continue along the A.T. for 1.2 miles to the junction with the blue-blazed side trail that leads right .1 mile to Chimney Rocks. To the left, the blue-blazed trail continues to Hermitage Cabin.

From here, you can either retrace your steps south on the A.T. back to Antietam Road or make a loop hike of the day trip by taking the side trail to Hermitage Cabin and Tumbling Run Shelter. The side trail adds only .25 mile or so to the total mileage of the trip.

Trailhead Directions
From Pennsylvania 16 just north of the town of Blue Ridge Summit, take a right on Rattlesnake Run Road. Rattlesnake Run Road intersects Antietam (Old Forge) Road just north of the A.T. crossing. Take a right on Antietam Road and follow it to the trail crossing.

MARYLAND

MARYLAND

The Applachian Trail follows the ridge of South Mountain through Maryland for more than 40 miles and descends to the Potomac River at Harpers Ferry, West Virginia. From Pen Mar Park in the north to Weverton Cliffs in the south, the trail in Maryland is steeped in history, particularly concerning the Civil War era.

The A.T. passes by High Rock, Buzzard Knob, Black Rock Cliffs, Annapolis Rocks, Monument Knob, White Rocks, Crampton Gap and Weverton Cliffs. Of particular historical note are Washington Monument State Park, Turners Gap with the South Mountain Inn, Crampton Gap with Gathland State Park, and the town of Weverton.

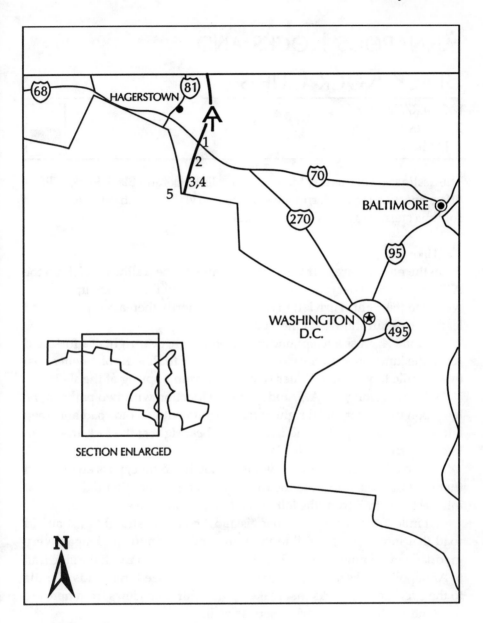

1. Annapolis Rocks and Black Rock Cliffs
2. White Rocks
3. Weverton Cliffs
4. Weverton Cliffs II
5. C&O Canal Towpath

Annapolis Rocks and Black Rock Cliffs

MODERATE
7.2 miles roundtrip
3 1/2 hours

The destination of this day hike—Annapolis Rocks and Black Rocks Cliff—offers spectacular western views of the Maryland countryside as well as southwestern views of Greenbrier Lake.

The Hike

From the parking area off US 40, hike .1 mile to the trailhead. Pick up the A.T. at the US 40 overpass, and follow a dirt road that climbs up into the woods to the right. Turn left in .1 mile, and shortly thereafter, pass a road leading to a farmhouse on the right.

At mile .4, cross a telephone line cut-through, bear right at a fork, and reach the junction with the side trail that leads to Pine Knob Shelter, just over .1 mile to your left. Water is available from a spring at the shelter.

Continue along the A.T. and reach the junction with two paths to the left. Soon thereafter, head right at the junction with an old road and keep left of the "island" just ahead. At mile .75, bear right at the fork and begin to climb steeply up through a laurel grove.

Reach a level crest just below Pine Knob in .25 mile, pass an old road that intersects the trail from the right and then pass another old road that intersects the trail from the left. From here, begin to descend steeply.

At mile 1, go around another "island," continue straight past an old road that intersects the trail to the right, and begin to climb again very gradually in .25 mile. At mile 1.8, go left at the fork and reach the side trail to Annapolis Rocks in another .5 mile. The blue-blazed trail leads .25 mile to the overhanging rocks that make up this cliff. The views from here are outstanding. There is a spring here as well.

When you return to the A.T., continue ahead and begin to descend in just over .5 mile. At mile 3.6, reach the side trail that leads a short distance to Black Rock Cliffs. The 180-degree view from this lookout point is outstanding, and you may want to note the considerable amount of scree at the bottom of the cliff.

From here, return to the parking area off US 40 by following the A.T. south.

Trailhead Directions
To get to the trailhead, take US 40 from Hagerstown to its first crossing over Interstate 70. The parking lot is immediately to your right after crossing the interstate. A blue-blazed trail leads to the A.T. from the parking area.

WHITE ROCKS

MODERATE
7 miles roundtrip
3 1/2 hours

The highlight of this hike is a small quartzite cliff known as White Rocks. The views offered at this overlook are poor in the summer but excellent in the late fall and winter. This hike begins at Crampton Gap in Gathland State Park, where there is a memorial to Civil War correspondents. A battle was also fought in the vicinity and the ruins of Gathland can still be seen.

Civil War Correspondent George Alfred Townsend, who used the pen name Gath, built his estate on South Mountain in 1884 with the proceeds from his war fiction and newspaper articles. He built a home, a hall, a library, a lodge, a guest house, a house for his wife, servants' quarters, a stable and a tomb for himself (although he was not buried in it). He named the estate Gathland after his pseudonym. Since 1884, all the buildings, though built of stone, have been vandalized to such a degree that only a wing of Gath Hall has been restored. This building now houses a museum, and restrooms, water, picnic tables and a telephone are all available in the park.

The memorial arch to Civil War correspondents and artists also remains intact. Framing the Catoctin Valley, the fifty-foot-tall memorial faces the battlefields of Winchester and Gettysburg. Inscriptions cover the arch, and mythological figures are carved into its stonework, but whether it is a cross between a Moorish arch and the old Frederick fire company station, or a reproduction of the front of the former Antietam Fire Company building, its origins remain a mystery. It was designed by Gath and is now administered by the National Park Service, whereas the 135-acre park is maintained by Maryland Department of Natural Resources.

The Hike

From Gapland Road (Maryland 225) also called Crampton Gap, in Gathland State Park, pass through a gap in a stone fence and cross a field. Heavy fighting occurred in this field during the Battle of Crampton's Gap on September 14, 1862. Shortly thereafter, pass the ruins of a large stone barn built in 1887 and some picnic tables. Climb up an old road and turn left off the road onto a path in .1 mile.

Join the old road in .25 mile, and in another .1 mile, reach the junction with a blue-blazed side trail that heads right .25 mile to Crampton Gap Shelter. At mile 1.7, reach an interesting knoll where, to your right, there is a pile of evenly fractured boulders. This is an excellent viewpoint in the winter.

From here, hike nearly .5 mile to another viewpoint from a large rockpile, which offers limited views of Elk Ridge and Pleasant Valley. The footing becomes rocky here as you continue to another winter view to your right at mile 2.3. Continue ahead through woods with heavy undergrowth, and at about mile 3, turn left at a trail junction and begin to climb. Ahead, the blue-blazed trail leads .25 mile to Bear Spring and another .5 mile to the locked Bear Spring Cabin.

Continue along the A.T., head straight at the fork in .1 mile, and soon thereafter, pass a rock outcropping to your right. Turn left at a trail junction in another .25 mile. Note the azaleas, red maples and chestnuts here.

A short distance later, reach the junction with the side trail that leads to White Rocks. Hike a very short distance along the blue-blazed trail to the quartzite cliffs, which offer excellent views in the winter.

From here, return south to Crampton Gap via the A.T.

Trailhead Directions

From US Alt. 40, take Maryland 67 South (from the west) or Maryland 17 South (from the east). Then take Gapland Road (Maryland 572), which you will follow to the parking lot in Gathland State Park. (Maryland 67 North and Maryland 17 North can be reached from US 340.)

WEVERTON CLIFFS

MODERATE
8.8 miles roundtrip
4 1/2 hours

An easy hike on this ridgetop section of trail, with a few short, steep descents and climbs, takes you to a spectacular view of the Potomac River Gorge from the rock outcropping at Weverton Cliffs. This is the most popular section of trail in Maryland, with the possible exception of a .1-mile piece in Washington Monument Park. Weverton Cliffs can get crowded on pleasant summer days, but the walk is just as pretty in the early spring and late fall or winter if you are interested in some solitude. The plaque at Weverton Cliffs remembers Congressman Goodloe E. Byron, who was a longtime supporter of the A.T.

The Hike
From the trailhead on Maryland 67, walk along the road to Brownsville and turn left onto the town's main street. Take your next right on a paved road marked Brownsville Pass. As you climb the ridge, the road turns to dirt and joins the A.T. at Brownsville Gap at about mile 1.

When you reach the A.T., turn right and hike south along the ridge for 1.5 miles. Reach the junction with a short, blue-blazed side trail that leads to a viewpoint at mile 2.5. Continue following the A.T. along the top of South Mountain, and cross or follow a couple of old roads.

At mile 3.3, start a short, steep descent at the southern end of South Mountain and reach the junction with the .1-mile blue-blazed trail to Weverton Cliffs in .75 mile.

To return, hike north on the A.T. to Brownsville Gap and follow the road back to the trailhead in Brownsville, Maryland.

Trailhead Directions
From US 340, just north of crossing the Potomac River into Maryland, follow Maryland 67 north to Brownsville. Park at the picnic area next to the access road to Brownsville.

WEVERTON CLIFFS II

STRENUOUS
2 miles roundtrip
1 1/2 hours

This hike is a steep climb but rewards you with a spectacular view of the Potomac River Gorge from the rock outcropping at Weverton Cliffs. This is the most popular section of trail in Maryland, with the possible exception of a .1-mile piece in Washington Monument Park. Weverton Cliffs can get crowded on pleasant summer days, but the walk is just as pretty in the early spring and late fall or winter if you are interested in some solitude. The plaque at Weverton Cliffs remembers Congressman Goodloe E. Byron, who was a longtime supporter of the A.T.

The Hike
From the trailhead, follow the A.T. north. The climb is steep and involves switchbacks. Reach the cliffs at mile 1.

Trailhead Directions
To reach the trailhead at Weverton Road, follow Maryland 67 North from US 340. Weverton Road is the first right turn after US 340. Parking is available alongside the trail. The A.T. crosses Weverton Road 1 mile from Maryland 67.

C & O CANAL TOWPATH

EASY
5.4 miles roundtrip
2 1/2 hours

A leisurely stroll will take you from historic Harpers Ferry, West Virginia, over the Potomac River into Maryland for a nice walk along the Chesapeake & Ohio Canal Towpath. The Canal once provided a means to bypass the rapids on the Potomac River, which had blocked the flow of goods by river. The long abandoned Towpath served as a vital link connecting towns along the Potomac with Washington D.C. Built in the late 1700s and early 1800s, it ran 185 miles from Cumberland, Maryland, to Georgetown, on the edge of the nation's capital city.

The hike is listed as a 5.4 mile roundtrip, but that takes you to the A.T.'s other junction with the Towpath. It is only .25 mile from Harpers Ferry to the Towpath, itself, and roundtrip hikes as short as .5 mile are possible. This is a good area to stretch your legs and enjoy a walk along the river. Hike as much of the Towpath as you like, leaving time for the return trip.

The Hike

From the John Brown's Fort in Harpers Ferry, West Virginia, follow the white blazes on the brown posts that lead to the Goodloe Byron Memorial Footbridge over the Potomac River. On the Maryland side of the Potomac, descend by stairs to the C & O Towpath. Turn to the right and follow the A.T. and C & O Towpath, which share the same footpath for the next 2.6 miles. Hike out as far along the A.T./C & O Towpath as you like.

Retrace your steps to return to Harpers Ferry.

Trailhead Directions

Park in the National Park Service parking area in Harpers Ferry, West Virginia. The parking fee is $5 per car. The trailhead is down Shenandoah Street from the parking area at the replica of the fire hall, where John Brown made his last stand during his 1859 raid on the Federal Arsenal.

WEST VIRGINIA

VIRGINIA

WEST VIRGINIA/VIRGINIA

The Appalachian Trail in West Virginia is about 3 miles and is centered in the town of Harpers Ferry, which is also home to the Appalachian Trail Conference Headquarters. The A.T. also passes through West Virginia further south when the trail travels in southern Virginia along the border of the two states. Here, the trail traverses Peters Mountain north of Pearisburg, Virginia.

The longest stretch of the A.T. is in Virginia, which comprises more than a quarter of the A.T.'s length. From the Potomac River near Harpers Ferry, the A.T. ridge hops westward along the Blue Ridge until it reaches Shenandoah National Park. It traverses the park for more than 100 miles, leaving the park behind at Rockfish Gap, and picking up the Blue Ridge Parkway, which it more or less parallels for 100 miles until the Roanoke area. Along the parkway, it traverses Humpback Mountain, Three Ridges, The Priest, Spy Rock, Punchbowl and Bluff Mountains, and then descends to the James River. From the James River, the trail climbs to Apple Orchard Mountain, the highest point on the Blue Ridge Parkway in Virginia.

In Troutville/Cloverdale, the A.T. leaves the Parkway and heads west toward the border of West Virginia. As it crosses this area, it passes by the remarkable features of Tinker Cliffs, MacAfee Knob, Dragons Tooth and the Audie Murphy Monument. The crest of Peters Mountain traverses the Virginia/West Virginia border. From here, the A.T. descends to Pearisburg, climbs Angels Rest on Pearis Mountain, and for the next 85 miles, slowly winds its way back toward Interstate 81, though not before crossing Interstate 77 near Bastian, Virginia.

From Atkins, Virginia, the A.T. heads south into the Mount Rogers National Recreation Area, passing through Grayson Highlands and within .5 mile of the summit of Mount Rogers, Virginia's highest point. From Mount Rogers, it is 30 miles to the Virginia/Tennessee state line. In this southern section of Virginia, the trail traverses White Top Mountain, Buzzard Rock and Straight Mountain before descending into the hiker-friendly town of Damascus, Virginia. Damascus holds an annual Trail Days festival each May. The state line is 3 miles south of Damascus.

About 100 miles of the Appalachian Trail in Virginia pass through Shenandoah National Park. The park is one of the most popular areas to hike along the A.T. Established by President Coolidge in 1926, Shenandoah National Park took ten years to complete. Most of the work was done by President Roosevelt's CCC; it was dedicated by Roosevelt in 1936. The parkway—Skyline Drive—was also part of the original concept, and took eight years to complete. Beginning construction in 1931, the southern, central and northern sections opened as they were completed (1939, 1934 and 1936, respectively).

Although the A.T. was first constructed through the Shenandoahs in the 1920s and opened in 1929, much of the trail was relocated as Skyline Drive was built. The CCC was also put to work rebuilding the A.T. and you will note the laborious rock work that shores up much of the trail in the park.

The history of the Shenandoahs—natural, geologic, cultural—can and does fill books. For additional information on the park, look for books sold at the park's visitor centers. The flora and fauna of the park is varied and includes everything from black bear and white-tailed deer (the latter, extremely prevalent) to the less often seen puma, mountain lions and bobcats. The areas of intense defoliation you will see have been caused by the gypsy moth. The deer tick is also present in the Shenandoahs, so search your body carefully for this carrier of Lyme Disease. As for flora, everything from hemlock-hardwood forests to boreal forests can be found in the Shenandoahs. Flowers and flowering shrubs also abound, making the park a fairyland walk from late spring through mid summer.

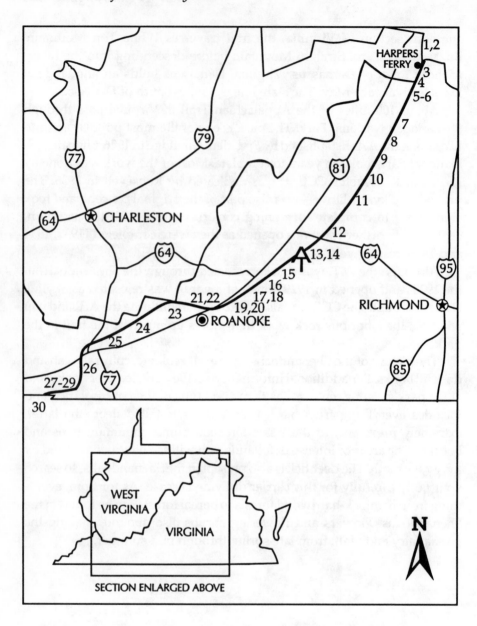

1. Loudon Heights Loop
2. Harpers Ferry
3. Buzzard Rock
4. Devils Racecourse
5. Bears Den Rocks
6. Bears Den Rocks and Lookout Point
7. Compton Gap and Compton Peak
8. North Marshall Mountain
9. Stony Man and Little Stony Man Loop
10. Bearfence Mountain Loop
11. Blackrock
12. Calf Mountain
13. Humpback Rocks
14. Humpback Rocks and Humpback Mountain
15. Hanging Rock
16. Spy Rock
17. Cold Mountain
18. Brown Mountain Creek
19. Bluff Mountain
20. Apple Orchard Mountain and The Guillotin
21. McAfee Knob
22. Dragon's Tooth
23. Wind Rock
24. Dismal Creek Falls
25. Chestnut Knob
26. Comers Creek Cascades
27. Rhododendron Gap
28. Mount Rogers
29. Buzzard Rock
30. Straight Mountain

LOUDON HEIGHTS LOOP

MODERATE
6.9 mile loop
4 hours

The Loudon Heights Loop offers several outstanding views as well as a walk through the historic town of Harpers Ferry. The Loudon Heights Trail creates a loop with the A.T. and takes you through three states—Maryland, West Virginia and Virginia.

For more than 1 mile of the hike, the A.T. follows the old Chesapeake & Ohio Canal Towpath. The Canal once provided a means to bypass the rapids on the Potomac River, which had blocked the flow of goods by river. The now abandoned Towpath served as a vital commercial link, connecting towns along the Potomac with Washington D.C. Built in the late 1700s and early 1800s, it ran the 185 miles from Cumberland, Maryland, to Georgetown, on the edge of the nation's capital city.

At the end of the hike, you will pass the replica of the fire hall where John Brown's followers made their last stand. John Brown was seeking to start a slave uprising when he made his 1859 raid on the federal arsenal at Harpers Ferry. He was captured and later hanged for treason. A number of interpretive displays in the town explain the raid and its consequences in detail.

During your visit to Harpers Ferry, drop by the Appalachian Trail Conference Headquarters located at the corner of Washington and Jackson streets just up the hill from the A.T. The headquarters visitors center is open seven days a week during the summer months.

The Hike
From the trailhead on the corner of Washington and Shenandoah Streets in Harpers Ferry, follow the A.T. up Washington Street and immediately turn left. The trail climbs old stone steps up from the street. Pass to the right of St. Peter's Roman Catholic Church and then to the left of the ruins of St. John's Episcopal Church. At mile .25, reach a fork in the path. To the left is Jefferson Rock, a boulder on top of another large rock that is a popular climbing spot for children. The view from the rock is tremendous.

Follow the right fork marked by "Harper Cemetery" sign and ascend on some remarkable stone steps put in by the ATC's volunteer trail crew in

1993, reaching the junction with a .25-mile blue-blazed side trail in .25 mile. The trail passes through the National Park Service's Mather Training Center (formerly Storer College) and leads to the Appalachian Trail Conference Headquarters on the corner of Washington and Jackson Streets.

Hike another .25 mile to US 340. Turn left and walk, facing traffic, on the sidewalk across the bridge over the Shenandoah River. This road crossing is perhaps the most dangerous section on the A.T. Although no injuries have occured, cars and trucks are often going 50-60 mph. Use caution. (*NOTE:* A relocation has been planned to route the A.T. under the bridge. Keep an eye out for blazes.)

Cross the road, and enter the woods to the right, ascending stairs up a cliff. Climb up Loudon Heights and cross West Virginia 32 at mile 1.7; cross and follow old roads as you continue to climb. Reach the top of the ridge at mile 2.3, and the junction with the blue-blazed Loudon Heights Trail.

Turn left and follow the Loudon Heights Trail, passing stone breast-works built by Federal infantrymen during the Civil War. At mile 3.1, reach the short side trail leading to a spectacular view of Harpers Ferry and the confluence of the Shenandoah and Potomac Rivers. Hike another .25 mile and pass under power lines in a cleared utility right-of-way. Reach the junction with a short side trail leading to a fine view of the rivers below in another .5 mile. Descend, sometimes steeply, off the ridge for .4 mile to a dirt road. Turn left on the road, then right onto a path.

Reach U.S. 340 at mile 4.4, and the junction with Virginia 671 at mile 4.7. Follow the walkway across the Sandy Hook Bridge as it crosses the Potomac River. On the far side of the bridge, the Loudon Heights Trail follows an old road to Sandy Hook Road. At mile 5.4, turn right onto paved Sandy Hook Road and reach the junction with the A.T. in .1 mile.

Follow the A.T. south along the C&O Towpath. Reach the Goodloe Byron Memorial Footbridge in 1.1 miles. Climb up to the bridge on stairs and cross the Potomac River. At the far end of the bridge, you will enter the town of Harpers Ferry. Follow the white blazes and signs. The trailhead at Washington and Shenandoah Streets is .1 mile beyond the bridge.

Trailhead Directions

Take your first right off of US 340 after crossing the Shenandoah River from Virginia into West Virginia. There is a sign for Harpers Ferry National Historic Park. Park in the dirt parking area on the right. The A.T. crosses the Shenandoah River on US 340. Look for the white-blazed A.T. leading into the woods across the road from the dirt parking area.

HARPERS FERRY

EASY
2 miles roundtrip
1 hour

The A.T. passes through the town of Harpers Ferry, by several areas of historic interest, and offers some fine views of the Shenandoah and Potomac Rivers. You will hike to Jefferson Rock, where you will find a fine view of the confluence of the Shenandoah and Potomac Rivers. The trail takes you past the ruins of St. John's Episcopal Church and St. Peter's Roman Catholic Church, a fine old stone church whose steeple dominates the Harpers Ferry "skyline;" it is still in use. The trail descends on stone steps to the streets of Harpers Ferry and passes by John Brown's "fort" on the way to the Potomac River.

John Brown was seeking to start a slave uprising when he made his 1859 raid on the Federal arsenal at Harpers Ferry. He was later hanged for treason. A number of interpretive displays in the town explain the raid and its consequences in detail.

During your visit to Harpers Ferry, you should drop by the Appalachian Trail Conference Headquarters. They are at the corner of Washington and Jackson Streets just up the hill from the A.T. The headquarters visitors center is open seven days a week during the summer months.

The Hike

From the trailhead at US 340, hike north on the A.T. and begin climbing. At mile .25, reach the junction with a side trail leading .25 mile to the Appalachian Trail Conference headquarters. This side trail passes through the National Park Service's Mather Training Center.

Reach a fork in .25 mile, and follow the right branch. At mile .75, pass the side trail to Jefferson Rock. It is a boulder on top of another large rock that is a popular climbing spot for children. The view from the rock is tremendous.

Continue north on the A.T. and pass the ruins of St. John's Episcopal Church on your left. Less than .1 mile beyond the ruins of the St. John's, pass St. Peter's Roman Catholic Church to your right and descend stone steps to Washington Street in Harpers Ferry. Turn right on Washington Street and immediately left onto Shenandoah Street.

In one block, Shenandoah Street deadends and the trail turns right, passing to the right of the fire hall, which is a replica of John Brown's fort. The trail follows the brick walkway around to the right and reaches the Byron Goodloe Memorial Bridge at mile 1.

The return hike is back south on the A.T. to the trailhead at US 340.

Trailhead Directions
Take the first right off of US 340 after crossing the Shenandoah River from Virginia into West Virginia. There is a sign for Harpers Ferry National Historic Park. Park in the dirt parking area on the right. The A.T. crosses the Shenandoah River on US 340. Look for the white-blazed A.T. leading into the woods across the road from the dirt parking area.

BUZZARD ROCK

MODERATE
7.2 miles roundtrip
3 1/2 hours

Climbing gradaully out of Keys Gap, the trail leads to a spectacular view from Buzzard Rock. Shannondale Lake can be seen in the foreground and the Shenandoah River at Avon Bend, just beyond it to the west.

The Hike
From the trailhead at Keys Gap, hike south on the A.T. Cross two old roads and reach the David Lesser Memorial Shelter at mile 2.4. A few short, steep climbs along the ridge will bring you to Buzzard Rock at mile 3.6.

The return hike is back north on the A.T. to the trailhead at Keys Gap.

Trailhead Directions
The parking area on Virginia 9 at Keys Gap is 6 miles east of Hillsboro, Virginia, and 7.4 miles west of Charles Town, West Virginia.

DEVILS RACECOURSE

MODERATE
6.4 miles roundtrip
3 1/2 hours

Devils Racecourse, the destination of this hike, is an ancient streambed with only the boulders remaining. While day hiking along the Blue Ridge in Northern Virginia, you will find excellent views of the Shenandoah and Shenandoah River Valley from Crescent Rock, .5 mile before reaching Devils Racecourse.

Although this hike begins in Virginia, about half of this section of the A.T. is located in Jefferson County, West Virginia.

The Hike
From the A.T. sign in the median strip of Virginia 7, follow Virginia 679 north for a short distance, turn right, and climb into a woods of laurel, pine and chestnut oak. Reach a rock outcropping at mile .6 mile, where you will find good views of the valley and then descend through rocks (sometimes steeply and on switchbacks) for .25 mile to a stream crossing at Pigeon Hollow. Climb steeply and continue ahead when you reach the junction with an old path. At mile 1.1, hike through some woods.

Begin to climb steeply, then more moderately, through the woods, and reach a good view of the Shenandoah Valley at a quartzite rock outcropping to your left at mile 1.7. Soon thereafter, begin to descend gradually, then more steeply through rocks. This particular area is notorious for its poison ivy. Watch out.

At just over mile 2, head left and continue to descend through a forest, and shortly thereafter, bear left again, cross a rocky creek bed, and pass a path to your right. Turn right at the next fork and reach the junction with a blue-blazed side trail to the left that heads to a spring (passing a poor spring, first). Rejoin the A.T. a short distance later.

Continue along the A.T. to where the side trail to the spring rejoins the trail in less than .1 mile, and begin a short ascent that can be slippery in wet or icy weather. At mile 2.5, head right at the fork, and shortly thereafter, reach Crescent Rock, where there are views of the Shenandoah River and Valley, and the Massanutten Mountains in the distance.

If you have the time, you may want to take the side trail that leads a short distance to a point where the cliff can be descended. If you walk back along the base of Crescent Rock, you can see the geological folds that give the rock its name. The core of the fold has been removed by the action of ice in the crevices, and a six-feet-deep arch has been formed in the cliff. About 150 feet west of Crescent Rock is another geological formation called Pulpit Rock (Pinnacle). This column of rock is separated from the cliff by about ten feet. Watch out for snakes in warm weather who enjoy sunning themselves on the exposed rocks.

Continue along the A.T., climb through a woods, and head left at a junction with an old road, which heads right .5 mile to parking at Virginia 601. The A.T. descends steeply ahead, bears right at a fork, leaves the old road, and arrives at Devils Racecourse. Listen carefully for the small stream that still runs beneath this ancient stream deposit of boulders.

From here, return to the parking area by heading south on the A.T.

Trailhead Directions
There is a parking area at the southwest corner of Virginia 7 and Virginia 601 that can be used for this day hike. There is also room for several cars where the A.T. leaves Virginia 679. The trail crossing at Virginia 7 is west of Bluemont, Virginia.

BEARS DEN ROCKS

EASY
1.2 miles roundtrip
1 hour

Although brief, this day hike leads to excellent views of the Shenandoah Valley.

The Hike
From the median strip at Virginia 7 just west of Snickers Gap, head east for .1 mile and turn right onto a gravel driveway. The driveway becomes a footpath almost immediately and climbs .5 mile to Bears Den Rocks. A side trail to the left heads .25 mile to Bears Den Hostel.

From here, return north to Snickers Gap via the A.T.

Trailhead Directions

There is a parking area at the southwest corner of Virginia 7 and Virginia 601 that can be used for this day hike. There is also room for several cars where the A.T. leaves Virginia 679. The trail crossing at Virginia 7 is west of Bluemont, Virginia.

BEARS DEN ROCKS AND LOOKOUT POINT

MODERATE
6.2 miles roundtrip
3 1/2 hours

Excellent views of the Shenandoah Valley from Bears Den Rocks and Lookout Point are highlight of this day hike.

The Hike

From the median strip at Virginia 7 just west of Snickers Gap, head east for .1 mile and turn right onto a gravel driveway. The driveway becomes a footpath almost immediately and climbs .5 mile to Bears Den Rocks. A side trail to the left heads .25 mile to Bears Den Hostel.

Continue along the A.T., descend through pines, and reach a blue-blazed side trail that leads left a short distance to a spring at mile .9. At mile 1.2, cross a creek on a footbridge, and shortly thereafter, cross another stream where the pines end.

Next, cross an old road, continue through woods, and descend steeply at mile 2. The descent soon becomes more gradual and you will cross Spout Run in a narrow, steep ravine at mile 2.3. After crossing the run, cross a badly eroded old road, begin to climb steeply, and reach the ridge crest at mile 2.8.

The sparsely wooded crest has a dense undergrowth of weeds, briars and poison ivy. Watch your step. You will reach the peak of the ridge at mile 3, and Lookout Point shortly thereafter. Lookout Point boasts excellent views of the mountains to the south.

From here, return to Snickers Gap by retracing your footsteps north along the A.T.

Trailhead Directions

There is a parking area at the southwest corner of Virginia 7 and Virginia 601 that can be used for this day hike. There is also room for several cars where the A.T. leaves Virginia 679. The trail crossing at Virginia 7 is west of Bluemont, Virginia.

COMPTON GAP TO COMPTON PEAK
Shenandoah National Park

MODERATE
2 miles roundtrip
1 hour

The highlights of this hike to the summit of Compton include good views and an interesting rock formation of columnar basalt.

The Hike
From Compton Gap at Skyline Drive Milepost 10.4 (elevation 2,415 feet), head south on the A.T. and climb Compton Mountain via switchbacks. In mid May, you may see yellow lady's-slippers blooming trailside, in early June, white clintonia and speckled wood lily.

At mile .75, reach a signpost at the junction of a blue-blazed trail that heads left and right to viewpoints (these trails are ungraded and rough but are worth the short trip to the viewpoints).

Follow the blue-blazed trail on the left .25 mile to an interesting rock formation composed of columnar basalt. To see this structure, you must climb below the rocks. At the top of the rock outcropping, you will find spectacular views to the west and north of Page Valley and the Shenandoah River.

Return to the A.T. and follow the blue-blazed trail right to the summit of Compton Peak (elevation 2,909 feet). You can continue another .25 mile beyond the peak to a rocky ledge with more good views to the west and north.

Return to Compton Gap by retracing your footsteps north on the A.T.

Trailhead Directions
The parking area at Compton Gap is located south of Front Royal, Virginia, at mile 10.4 of Skyline Drive.

North Marshall Mountain

Shenandoah National Park

MODERATE
1.2 miles roundtrip
1 hour

The summit of North Marshall Mountain (elevation 3,368 feet) is the destination of this day hike. This mountain, and its sister, South Marshall, were named for John Marshall, Chief Justice of the United States from 1801-1835. These mountains were once part of Marshall's Blue Ridge holdings.

The Hike
From the paved parking area at Skyline Drive (elevation 3,087 feet), head north on the A.T. and climb North Marshall Mountain via switchbacks. The trail turns sharply left as it nears the summit, where you will find high cliffs to the right. If you are interested in rock scrambling, the cliffs make an excellent addition to the hike.

Continue along the A.T., and at the next bend, enjoy an excellent view of Blue Ridge to the south. Reach the crest of the ridge at mile .5. The cliffs to the left of the trail offer outstanding views to the west. Hike another .1 mile to the summit of North Marshall.

From here, return to the parking area at Skyline Drive by heading south on the A.T.

Trailhead Directions
The parking area is located south of Front Royal, Virginia, at Milepost 15.9 on Skyline Drive.

STONY MAN AND LITTLE STONY MAN LOOP

Shenandoah National Park

MODERATE
3 mile loop
2 hours

This hike will take you over the ancient lava flows that once formed the Shenandoah Mountains. The profile of Stony Man, which can be seen from Skyline Drive, was formed by the erosion of layers of lava. You will loop the summit of Stony Man and pass below the towering Little Stony Man Cliffs. This day hike uses the A.T. (which shares its path with the Stony Man Nature Trail on this section), the Passamaquoddy Trail, and the Stony Man Horse Trail.

The Passamaquoddy Trail was the route the A.T. followed until 1990. The word Passamaquoddy is an Abenaki Indian word for "abounding in Pollock." The Maine Indian word was selected to honor George Pollock who layed out the trail in 1932.

The Hike

From the Stony Man Nature Trail Parking Area, hike north on the A.T. The A.T. shares the trailway on this section with the Stony Man Nature Trail. At mile .4, follow the loop trail straight ahead as the trail turns. Follow the loop trail for another .4 mile as it circles the summit of Stony Man. Return to the A.T. and continue hiking north. In .6 mile, reach the cliffs of Little Stony Man. The trail descends sharply and reaches the bottom of the cliffs in .25 mile.

At the base of the cliffs, reach the junction with the Passamaquoddy Trail. Turn back to the left and follow the blue-blazed trail, which passes beneath Little Stony Man Cliffs. Hike another 1 mile to the junction with the yellow-blazed Stony Man Horse Trail. Follow the yellow-blazed trail the .25 mile back to the Stony Man Nature Trail Parking Area.

Trailhead Directions

The Stony Man Nature Trail Parking Area is located south of Front Royal, Virginia, at Skyline Drive Milepost 41.7.

BEARFENCE MOUNTAIN LOOP
Shenandoah National Park

MODERATE
1.5 mile loop
1 hour

This short hike is not a true loop but rather a figure eight. You will hike over a very rough section of trail to the rocky top of Bearfence Mountain, which offers fine views of Skyline Drive, the surrounding mountains and the valley. The Bearfence Mountain Loop is listed here as a moderate hike because it is short, but the climbs involve using your hands, as well as your feet, to scramble over the rocks. In the summer, naturalist-led hikes of the area leave from the parking area. If you are interested in a naturalist-led hike, check with the park for times and dates.

The Hike
From the Bearfence Mountain Parking Area, follow the blue-blazed trail across the road from the parking area. In .1 mile, reach junction with the A.T., but continue following the blue-blazed trail (you will return on the A.T.). In the next .25 mile, the trail will climb up to and pass over a rough and rocky ridge on the north slope of Bearfence Mountain, where there are fine views from the ridgetop.

The blue-blazed trail joins the Bearfence Mountain Loop Trail at its junction with the A.T. Continue following the blue-blazed trail and climb to the summit of Bearfence Mountain(elevation 3,500 feet). The Bearfence Trail then descends to its second junction with the A.T. Turn back to the right on the white-blazed A.T., and in .25 mile, reach the junction with the Bearfence Mountain Loop Trail. Continue following the A.T., and in another .25 mile, reach the junction with the blue-blazed trail leading .1 mile to the parking area at the trailhead. Turn right and follow the blue-blazed trail back to the parking area.

Trailhead Directions
The Bearfence Mountain Parking Area is located north of Waynesboro, Virginia, at Skyline Drive Milepost 56.4.

BLACKROCK

SHENANDOAH NATIONAL PARK

MODERATE
2 miles roundtrip
1 hour

This short hike leads to outstanding views from Blackrock. The trail nearly circles the mountain as it passes around its north, west and south side.

The Hike

From the parking area at the trailhead, hike a short distance of the Jones Run Trail to the junction with the A.T. Turn right on the A.T. and hike south for .25 mile to Skyline Drive. Cross Skyline Drive and continue following the A.T., climbing gradually.

Pass around the summit of Blackrock (elevation 3,100 feet). There are several fine views from this section of trail. The return hike is back north on the A.T. to the Jones Run Trail, which leads to the parking area.

Trailhead Directions

The Jones Run Parking Area is located north of Waynesboro, Virginia, at Skyline Drive Milepost 83.8.

CALF MOUNTAIN

SHENANDOAH NATIONAL PARK

MODERATE
1.8 miles roundtrip
1 hour

On this day hike, the A.T. climbs gently up from Beagle Gap to the open summit of Calf Mountain, which offers fine views. Calf Mountain is a popular spot for watching hawks during their fall migration.

The Hike

From the trailhead at Beagle Gap, start climbing on the same side of the road as the dirt parking area. Hiking north on the A.T., you will ascend the southern slope of Little Calf Mountain. In .25 mile, reach a high point on the ridge between Little Calf Mountain and Calf Mountain. Continue hiking along the ridge, and in .6 mile, reach the open summit of Calf Mountain (elevation 2,974 feet).

The return hike is south on the A.T. to Beagle Gap.

Trailhead Directions
Beagle Gap has a small dirt lot for parking located north of Waynesboro, Virginia, at Milepost 99.5 of Skyline Drive.

HUMPBACK ROCKS

MODERATE
1.8 miles roundtrip
1 1/2 hours

This short hike will take you from the Blue Ridge Parkway to the top of Humpback Rocks. The hike up is very steep in some places and is much more difficult than many of the leg-stretcher type hikes that can be found along the Parkway. The destination is a jagged rock outcropping with fine views. Due to its location on the Blue Ridge Parkway, this hike is popular and can be very crowded on weekends in the summer.

Humpback Rocks was an important landmark on the Old Howardsville Turnpike. The Turnpike was a major trade road that connected the Rockfish and Shenandoah Valleys in the 1800s. The trace of the old turnpike is still very much in evidence where it crossed the Parkway just north of the Humpback Rocks Picnic Area.

The Hike
From the parking area, follow the signs and hike south on the A.T. The steady and sometimes steep climb up switchbacks will take you to a trail junction at mile .75. Turn left on this side trail, leaving the A.T. behind, and hike .1 mile to the top of Humpback Rocks.

Return to the trail junction and follow the A.T. north to the parking area near the Parkway.

Trailhead Directions
The Humpback Rocks parking area is located south of Waynesboro, Virginia, at Blue Ridge Parkway Milepost 6. The A.T. skirts the backside of the parking area, passing by the picnic table.

HUMPBACK ROCKS AND HUMPBACK MOUNTAIN

MODERATE
3.6 miles roundtrip
3 hours

This hike will take you from the Blue Ridge Parkway to the top of Humpback Rocks and the summit of Humpback Mountain. The hike up to the Rocks is very steep in some places and is much more difficult than many of the leg-stretcher type hikes that can be found along the Parkway. The destination is a jagged rock outcropping with fine views. Due to its location on the Blue Ridge Parkway, this hike is popular and can be very crowded on weekends in the summer.

Humpback Rocks was an important landmark on the Old Howardsville Turnpike. The Turnpike was a major trade road that connected the Rockfish and Shenandoah Valleys in the 1800s. The trace of the old turnpike is still very much in evidence where it crossed the Parkway just north of the Humpback Rocks Picnic Area.

The summit of Humpback Mountain offers good views of the surrounding area, and is less crowded than Humpback Rocks.

The Hike
From the parking area, follow the signs and hike south on the A.T. The steady and sometimes steep climb up switchbacks will take you to a trail junction at mile .75. Turn left on the side trail, leaving the A.T. behind, and hike .1 mile the top of Humpback Rocks.

Return to the trail junction, and continue following the A.T. south. The trail will continue a steady, and sometimes steep ascent for 1 mile to a cliff at the summit of Humpback Mountain (elevation 3,600 feet).

The return hike is north on the A.T. to the parking area near the Parkway.

Trailhead Directions
The Humpback Rocks parking area is located south of Waynesboro, Virginia, at Blue Ridge Parkway Milepost 6. The trail skirts the backside of the parking area, passing by the picnic table.

Hanging Rock

MODERATE 7.4 miles roundtrip 4 1/2 hours	

Along this hike you will pass over the summit of Bee Mountain, which offers limited views. At Hanging Rock, the destination of this day hike, you will be treated to fine views of two nearby mountains—Three Ridges (which Hanging Rock is located on) and The Priest.

The Hike

From Reeds Gap, hike south on the A.T. At mile 1.6, reach Maupin Field Shelter at the A.T.'s junction with the Mau-Har Trail. Continue following the A.T. south for .4 mile to the summit of Bee Mountain (elevation 3,000 feet). The trail then descends to a gap and begins climbing along the northern slope of Three Ridges. At mile 3.7, reach Hanging Rock (elevation 3,400 feet).

The return hike is back north on the A.T. to Reeds Gap.

Trailhead Directions

Reeds Gap is located at the intersection of Virginia 664 and the Blue Ridge Parkway at Milepost 13.6.

Spy Rock

MODERATE 6.6 miles roundtrip 3 1/2 hours	

The dome-shaped Spy Rock offers a magnificent panoramic view of the Religious Range, The Priest, Little Priest, The Friar, Little Friar and The Cardinal, as well as Maintop Mountain, Whetstone Ridge and Fork Mountain. This viewpoint was used by lookouts during the Civil War.

The Hike

From Crabtree Farm Road (Virginia 826), take the A.T. south and ascend through an open field. Look back to see Three Ridges and the mountains surrounding it. Hike .25 mile to the crest (elevation 3,480 feet) where you will descend .25 mile to an old lumber road that leads to Cash Hollow Road.

From this sag, ascend again and reach a level crest in .6 mile. Follow the crest for .25 mile, and pass through a rhododendron thicket at mile 1.8. In another .25 mile, reach the ridge (elevation 3,500 feet), continue along it for .25 mile, and descend through mountain laurel. At mile 2.4, enter private property, and .25 mile later, pass a rocky overhang to your left.

Begin your ascent of Maintop Mountain in .1 mile, and reach the wooded summit (elevation 4,040 feet) at mile 3. Pass a side trail that heads right to a view at a rock outcropping in .1 mile, and at mile 3.3, at the saddle of the mountain, reach the junction with a short side trail that leads to Spy Rock.

To the northwest is Great Valley, to the north, Maintop Mountain. Clockwise from Maintop are Pinnacle Ridge, The Priest, Little Priest, The Friar, Porters Ridge, The Cardinal, Pompey Mountain, Mount Pleasant, Cold Mountain, Tar Jacket Ridge, Rocky Mountain, Elk Pond Mountain, Whetstone Ridge, Bald Mountain and Fork Mountain.

From here, return to the A.T. and retrace your steps north to Virginia 826.

Trailhead Directions
Virginia 826 (unpaved Crabtree Farm Road) can be reached from Virginia 56, 14.6 miles west of Virginia 151 in the Tye River Valley.

COLD MOUNTAIN

MODERATE
7 miles roundtrip
4 hours

Both Tar Jacket Ridge and Cold Mountains make this hike worthwhile. Panoramic views from both mountains are outstanding. From Tar Jacket Ridge, you can see Cold Mountain, Mount Pleasant, Pompey Mountain, The Friar, The Cardinal, The Priest and Maintop Mountain. From atop Cold Mountain, you can see Tar Jacket Ridge in the foreground, Rocky Mountain, Elk Pond Mountain, Spy Rock, Three Ridges, Little Priest, Bald Knob and all the mountains viewed from Tar Jacket Ridge.

Both Tar Jacket Ridge and Cold Mountain feature the remains of stone fences built prior to the Civil War. The former was named for a mountain man who tore his jacket on the ridge while running from angry bees. You may also see Cold Mountain referred to as Cole Mountain in some publications. That is due an error that worked its way into some government publications and has been referenced by other authors. Cold Mountain is how it is locally known.

The Hike
From Salt Log Gap at USFS 63 (also Virginia 634), follow the A.T. south. The elevation here is 3,247 feet. You will soon cross a woods road and begin to climb the northern slope of Tar Jacket Ridge.

In just over .5 mile, the A.T. heads left where an abandoned trail heads right. From here, climb gradually through open meadows and reach the crest of the trail along Tar Jacket Ridge in another .6 mile. The panoramic views of the mountains are magnificent, and from right to left are: Cold Mountain, Mount Pleasant, Pompey Mountain, The Friar, The Cardinal, The Priest and Maintop Mountain.

Continue along the A.T. for 1 mile the junction with a side trail that leads to a spring. A short distance later, reach a stile, cross USFS 48 at Hog Camp Gap (elevation 3,500 feet), and begin climbing south over Cold Mountain.

At Hog Camp Gap, USFS 48 heads right .5 mile to Wiggins Spring. To the left, USFS 48 heads 2.5 miles to Salt Log Gap. Also from the gap, a 5.3 mile blue-blazed circuit trail heads to Mount Pleasant and Pompey Mountain.

Hike .25 mile to steps and another .1 mile to a rock wall to the right, built as a boundary fence in the 1850s. Continue to climb Cold Mountain along switchbacks.

At mile 2.7, pass through a hickory grove, cross the access road again, and continue to your left. The northern end of Cold Mountain has been cleared and you will follow the road. Keep an eye out for the blazed rocks. At mile 3.3, take the right fork in the road, and .1 mile later, the next right fork.

At mile 3.5, reach the summit of Cold Mountain (elevation 4,022 feet). There is a granite rock to your left and outstanding views to the north and south. From left to right are: Rocky Mountain, Tar Jacket Ridge, Elk Pond Mountain, Maintop Mountain, Spy Rock, Three Ridges, The Priest, Little

Priest, The Cardinal, The Friar, Pompey Mountain and Mount Pleasant. Bald Knob is to the south.

From here, return to the parking area by following the A.T. north.

Trailhead Directions
Virginia 634 (USFS 63) at Salt Log Gap can be reached from US 60, 8.1 miles east of Buena Vista, or from U.S. 501, 4 miles east of Blue Ridge Parkway Milepost 45.6 and 18.3 miles east of Amherst and US 29. From U.S. 60, it is 7.1 miles along Virginia 634 (which becomes USFS 63) to the trail crossing.

BROWN MOUNTAIN CREEK

EASY
5.2 miles roundtrip
3 hours

Along the banks of Brown Mountain Creek, you will find old chimneys, rock walls and building foundations that recall a time in the 1800s when this creek was at the heart of a busy community. The little valley is now known for its tremendous wildflower display, which includes rhododendron, mountain laurel, showy orchis and a variety of ferns.

The Hike
From Long Mountain Wayside on US 60, hike south on the A.T. and descend into Brown Mountain Creek Valley. Hike 1 mile, and cross the creek for the first time. The trail follows alongside the creek for the remainder of the hike and it passes by old walls and foundations. At mile 1.8, reach the junction with the short side trail to Brown Mountain Creek Shelter. Water is available from two small springs. At mile 2.7, there is a footbridge over the creek. On the far side, the trail begins to climb again.

To return, climb north on the A.T. back up to the highway.

Trailhead Directions
The trailhead at US 60 is 17 miles west of Amherst, Virginia, and 9 miles east of Buena Vista, Virginia.

BLUFF MOUNTAIN

MODERATE
4 miles roundtrip
3 hours

The summit of Bluff Mountain offers only limited views, but the spruce-covered mountain top is a beautiful destination for a day hike. The summit also features a plaque in memory of Ottie Cline Powell, a youth who wandered away from school and died on the summit of Bluff Mountain. The plaque tells his sad tale.

You can also make a .5-mile side trip to Punchbowl Shelter, which has an idyllic setting on the side of a small pond. This relatively short day hike takes you up a steady climb of more than 1,100 feet. The ascent could be listed as strenuous, but the trail is graded well and the climb is only .25 mile.

The Hike

From the small parking area on the Blue Ridge Parkway, hike north on the A.T. and begin climbing the northeast slope of Punchbowl Mountain. At mile .4, reach the junction with the blue-blazed side trail, which leads .25 mile to Punchbowl Shelter. Continue on the A.T., and in .5 mile, reach the tree-covered summit of Punchbowl Mountain (elevation 2,848 feet).

Descend .25 mile to a gap and begin climbing Bluff Mountain. At mile 2, reach the wooded summit of Bluff Mountain. Note the plaque in memory of Ottie Cline Powell. Having just climbed to the summit yourself, you can appreciate why searchers never looked for the small boy here.

The return hike is north on the A.T. to the parking area.

Trailhead Directions

The parking area is at Blue Ridge Parkway Milepost 51.7, about 6 miles south of US 60 and about 12 miles north of US 501.

APPLE ORCHARD MOUNTAIN AND THE GUILLOTIN

EASY
3.9 miles roundtrip
2 hours

This unusual day hike takes you to the summit of Apple Orchard Mountain, which has a large FAA antenna on the top. The antenna is the only working remnant of Bedford Air Force Base, which operated on the summit from 1954 to 1974. As many as 120 airmen were stationed on the mountain during those twenty years.

A rock outcropping about .25 mile from the summit offers a fine view of the Great Valley of Virginia. Along the wooded trail up the mountain, trillium and other wildflowers abound along this section of the A.T. in the spring.

Half a mile from the summit of Apple Orchard, you will reach another highlight of this day hike—110 rock steps built by the Natural Bridge Appalachian Trail Club with help from the ATC's volunteer trail crew. The steps take the trail in and around several interesting rock formations, including The Guillotine, a large boulder that hangs over the trail, trapped in a cleft of another rock.

The Hike
From Sunset Field, follow the blue-blazed Apple Orchard Falls Trail as it descends .25 mile to the junction with the A.T. Turn right and follow the A.T. north, climbing up to FS 812 on steps. Cross the gravel road and again ascend on steps. The A.T. winds up the wooded side of Apple Orchard Mountain for the next 1.1 miles.

At mile 1.4, enter the field on the summit of the mountain, and reach the wooden post at the junction with the short side trail to the rock outcropping at mile 1.5. From the rock outcropping, return to the A.T. and continue hiking north to rock steps. Descend steps around rock formations and reach The Guillotine in .5 mile.

The return hike is south on the A.T. to the Apple Orchard Falls Trail, which you follow back to Sunset Field.

Trailhead Directions
Sunset Field is at Blue Ridge Parkway Milepost 78.4, 14.5 miles south of US 501 and 7.6 miles north of Virginia 43.

McAfee Knob

MODERATE
7 miles roundtrip
4 hours

McAfee Knob, an overhanging rock ledge with outstanding views, is the destination of this day hike. From the ledges, you can see both the Catawba and Roanoke Valleys, as well as the mountain ridges to the north and the west. To the right, view Tinker Cliffs, to the left, across the valley, view North Mountain, the former route of the A.T.

The Hike
From the parking area at Virginia 311, head north on the A.T. by crossing the road (carefully because southbound traffic has limited visibility), and pass under two utility lines. Turn left and begin to climb ridge along switchbacks.

Hike .25 mile to the crest of the ridge, bear right, and climb along an old woods road for .1 mile; follow the rocky crest of the ridge to your right. Begin to descend, heading right, and rejoin the old woods road. Turn right, leave the road, and arrive at bulletin board (to your left).

A sharp left turn will bring you parallel to the crest of the ridge, and for the next 1.5 miles, follow the ridge with minor ups and downs. In the fall and winter, Fort Lewis Mountain can be seen to your right. At mile 1, pass the Boy Scout Shelter a short distance off the trail to your right. The spring in front of the shelter is often dry in the summer.

At mile 1.9, turn right onto another old road, begin to descend, and shortly thereafter, reach the junction with a blue-blazed trail that heads left to a spring. After crossing a stream, pass a couple of blue-blazed trails on your right that lead to the Catawba Mountain Shelter.

Shortly thereafter, turn left off the woods road and begin to climb for .25 mile, cross a road, and pass through an area of thick laurel growth. Pass under a powerline in another .25 mile, turn right, and begin to climb up McAfee Knob. From the rock outcroppings to your left, you will find good winter views of the Catawba Valley, Gravelly Ridge and North Mountain. At mile 3.3, turn left onto an old road and continue to climb past large boulders. Many trails criss-cross this area, so keep an eye out for the white blazes marking the A.T. At a small clearing at the end of the road, a side trail heads left to the cliffs at McAfee Knob.

Return to the parking area by retracing your footsteps south on the A.T.

Trailhead Directions
Virginia 311 can be reached from Interstate 81 near Roanoke-Salem. The trail crossing is 8 miles north of Salem and 12 miles north of downtown Roanoke.

DRAGON'S TOOTH

MODERATE
5.2 miles roundtrip
3 hours

This day hike icludes viewpoints from Rawies Rest, Viewpoint Rock, Devils Seat and Dragon's Tooth. Dragon's Tooth is the most spectacular of the viewpoints and is the ultimate destination of the hike. From this monolith, you can see Catawba Valley, McAfee Knob and Big Tinker Mountain. On especially clear days, you can even see the Peaks of Otter along the Blue Ridge Parkway to the east.

The Hike
From Virginia 311 (at the USFS parking lot), follow the blue-blazed trail that heads right (uphill) for .4 mile to the A.T. The other blue-blazed trail in the parking lot leads 1.5 miles to the A.T., but if you take this one you will miss Rawies Rest, Viewpoint Rock and Devils Seat. You can follow this trail back to the parking lot on the return trip for a slight change of scenery. Neither of the trails increase nor decrease the mileage of this hike.

Join the A.T. and ascend for .75 mile to a narrow ridge. Hike another .25 mile along the narrow, knife-edge, rocky rim that is called Rawies Rest. This scenic spot affords good views as it climbs the crest of the spur of Cove Mountain.

At mile 1.3, reach Viewpoint Rock, which offers views of the gap between North and Cove Mountains. Turn left, and in another .25 mile, the crest opens up a bit as it passes to the right of Devils Seat, a rocky outlook on the southern edge of the spur that affords views of Catawba Valley and the surrounding mountains.

Begin to descend into the sag called Lost Spectacles Gap and reach the junction with the blue-blazed side trail that leads 1.5 miles down to the USFS parking lot. As you climb out of the gap and across the eastern slope of Cove Mountain, you will have occasional views of Catawba Valley to your left. At mile 2.1, cross a rock slope over a narrow ledge.

Hike another .4 mile to your first view of Dragon's Tooth, and climb steeply over rocks to the crest of Cove Mountain. When you reach the crest, the A.T. heads right and crosses the summit of the mountain (elevation 3,050 feet) in .1 mile. Reach the junction with a blue-blazed side trail that heads left a short distance to Dragon's Tooth where the A.T. turns right toward the summit of Cove Mountain. The crown of the tooth can reached by climbing up a crack but take extra care in windy or wet weather.

To return to the parking area, follow the A.T. north to its junction with the blue-blazed side trail at Lost Spectacles Gap and follow the side trail to the parking lot; or continue another 1.1 miles on the A.T. to the side trail that you followed from the parking area, and follow it .4 mile to the parking area.

Trailhead Directions
The parking area on Virginia 311 is .4 mile west of the intersection of Virginia 311 and Virginia 624.

WIND ROCK

EASY	
.5 mile roundtrip	
1 hour	

A short hike on a woods road will bring you to Wind Rock, a fine viewpoint. This easy leg-stretcher is a good way to introduce your non-hiker friends to the A.T.

The Hike
From Salt Sulphur Turnpike, hike north on the A.T. Follow an old woods road up the mountain for .25 mile to Wind Rock (elevation 4,100 feet). Look to the north for a nice view of Stony Creek Valley.

The return hike is back down the A.T. to the Turnpike.

Trailhead Directions

From Newport, Virginia, travel about 2 miles on US 460 to Virginia 613 (locally known as Salt Sulphur Turnpike). In 6 miles, the Turnpike passes Mountain Lake, and in another 5.5 miles, the Turnpike reaches a highpoint between Big Mountain and Potts Mountain. Here, the A.T. crosses the gravel turnpike.

DISMAL CREEK FALLS

MODERATE
2.8 miles roundtrip
1 1/2 hours

On this hike to the broad cascade of Dismal Falls, you will pass through thick groves of rhododendron. This day hike is a good choice for mid June because the rhododendron is often at its peak. Dismal Creek is a popular trout stream.

The Hike

From the trailhead on Virginia 606, hike north on the A.T. and begin climbing Brushy Mountain. In .5 mile, the trail drops steeply into a gully and begins to climb again. At mile 1.1, reach the junction with the blue-blazed side trail to Dismal Creek Falls. Turn left on the side trail and hike another .25 mile to the overlook of the falls.

To return, hike back to the A.T. on the side trail, turn right on the A.T., and hike south to Virginia 606.

Trailhead Directions

The reach the trailhead, travel 12 miles east of Bland, Virginia, to the intersection of Virginia 606 and Virginia 42. The trailhead is .75 mile west of Virginia 42 on Virginia 606.

CHESTNUT KNOB

MODERATE
2.6 miles roundtrip
2 hours

The open summit of Chestnut Knob offers a commanding view of Burkes Garden and the surrounding countryside. Burkes Garden is an oval-shaped bowl of more than 20,000 acres that looks like a volcanic crater. It was actually carved by water eroding the underlying layer of limestone rock. Chestnut Knob is at the southwest corner of the Garden. One of the best views on the mountain is from the three-sided privy for Chestnut Knob Shelter, a stone cabin on the summit.

The community of Burkes Garden holds its Fall Festival on the last Saturday in September. A variety of homemade foods and crafts are on sale during the festival, which can be combined with a trip to the trail.

The Hike
From the parking area in Walker Gap, hike south on the A.T. and begin climbing Chestnut Knob. You will cross an old woods road and a gravel road on the climb up the knob. At mile 1.3, reach the open summit of Chestnut Knob (elevation 4,409 feet).

The return hike is back north on the A.T. to the gravel road in Walker Gap.

Trailhead Directions
From Virginia 42, about 10.5 miles west of Interstate 77, take Virginia 623 north into Burkes Garden. Virginia 623 is the only paved road in or out of the National and Virginia Rural Historical District. In Burkes Garden, turn left on Virginia 727 and travel just over 5 miles to where the gravel road deadends at Walker Gap.

COMERS CREEK CASCADES

EASY
2.4 miles roundtrip
1 1/2 hours

This easy hike leads to Comers Creek Cascades, where there is a nice swimming hole at the base of this small waterfall. In 1994, the Virginia Department of Transportation asked for public comment on a plan to build a four-lane highway through here. The V.D.O.T. plan would reroute 1.5 miles of Trail and turn this cascade into a roadside culvert. The A.T.C. and other groups were pushing an alternate route. By early 1995, no decision had been made.

The Hike
From the trailhead at Dickey Gap, follow the A.T. south. The trail from the gap to the falls is along the side of Iron Mountain, which is actually more of a ridge than a mountain. At mile 1.2, cross Comer Creek at the base of the ten-foot cascade.

The return hike is back north to the trailhead at Dickey Gap.

Trailhead Directions
From Marion, Virginia, travel about 12 miles south on Virginia 16 to the trailhead at Dickey Gap, where Virginia 650 intersects Virginia 16.

RHODODENDRON GAP

MODERATE
5.2 mile roundtrip
3 hours

This hike takes you through the heart of the Virginia Highlands—an area of breathtaking beauty. You will climb up to Wilburn Ridge and follow a loop trail along the ridge to Rhododendron Gap. Wilburn Ridge has rock outcroppings that afford many magnificent views, and Rhododendron Gap surrounds the trail with hundreds of acres of rhododendrons. The rhododendron are usually at the peak of there bloom between the third week in June and the first week in July. The vast garden in bloom is an awesome sight to see. This is not a secret spot, however, and the trail can be crowded during peak bloom, particularly on weekends. Rhododendron

Gap is also a great place to come pick blueberries in late August.

Grayson Highlands State Park is also home to free-ranging ponies, which are frequently seen along the A.T. The ponies are not really wild, but they should not be approached or attempted to ride. Some of the ponies are sold at auction during the park's fall festival. The festival is held annually during the last weekend in September.

The Hike
From the main park road at Massie Gap, hike .5 mile on the blue-blazed Rhododendron Trail to the A.T. Turn left and follow the A.T. south. Hike another .5 mile, cross a fence, leaving Grayson Highlands State Park behind and entering Jefferson National Forest. Reach the junction with a blue-blazed side trail in .25 mile. Follow the trail, which leads straight up and over Wilburn Ridge to rejoin the A.T. on the other side of the two highpoints on the ridge. After rejoining the A.T., continue south and descend to Rhododendron Gap. After looking around the gap (there is a nice view from the rocks), hike back north on the A.T., which bears left around the highpoints on Wilburn Ridge. At the junction with the Rhododendron Trail, turn right and return to the parking area on the Grayson Highlands State Park road at Massie Gap.

Trailhead Directions
From Interstate 81 near Marion, follow the signs to Grayson Highlands State Park. The park is just north of the North Carolina/Virginia line on US 58, 8 miles west of the community of Volney, Virginia. Once in the park, follow the main park road to the trailhead at Massie Gap.

Mount Rogers

STRENUOUS
8.6 miles roundtrip
5 1/2 hours

Mount Rogers, at 5,729 feet, is the highest point in Virginia. Named for William Barton Rogers, the first state geologist of Virginia, Mount Rogers was once known as Balsam Mountain. The summit of Mount Rogers supports the northernmost natural stand of Fraser Fir and boasts an annual rainfall average of 60 inches and snowfall average of 57 inches.

There are no views from the summit of Mount Rogers, but this fir-covered peak makes a wonderful picnic spot.

The Hike

From the parking area at Virginia 600 (elevation 4,434 feet), cross the road, pass through the gate, head left, and climb through a field toward Mount Rogers. Keep an eye out for blazes here.

At mile .25, reach the crest of the ridge, where you'll find good views. Hike another .25 mile, cross a fence on a stile, and enter the Lewis Fork Wilderness Area. The A.T. continues to climb Mount Rogers through woods.

At mile 1.8, reach the former site of the Deep Gap Shelter (elevation 4,900 feet). A spring is located just south of the shelter site; the Virginia Highlands Horse Trail also passes through here. The shelter is now on display at a park in Damascus, Virginia.

Hike another .25 mile, cross the Virginia Highlands Horse Trail, and turn right uphill. Here, the blue-blazed Elk Garden Trail heads left 4 miles to the USFS Grindstone Campground at Virginia 603.

Descend briefly and turn left. To your right, enjoy views from a fence surrounding an open meadow. Climb the southern slope of Mount Rogers, cross several streams, enter an overgrown field, and continue to climb. At mile 3.8, reach the junction with the blue-blazed side trail that leads .5 mile to the summit of Mount Rogers (elevation 5,729 feet).

From the summit, return to the A.T. and follow the trail south to the parking area at Virginia 600.

Trailhead Directions

The A.T. crossing on Virginia 600 is at Elk Garden, a parking area just south of Mount Rogers. Elk Garden is 3.4 miles north of US 58 and 3.5 miles south of Virginia 603.

BUZZARD ROCK

EASY	
1.4 miles roundtrip	
1 hour	

This short and relatively easy day hike takes you to stupendous views from Buzzard Rock atop Whitetop Mountain.

The Hike

From the parking area on Whitetop Mountain Road, turn left off the road onto the footpath that heads south to Buzzard Rock. As you descend through the open field, you will see your destination—a prominent rock peak. From Buzzard Rock, enjoy excellent views to the south and west.

Return to the parking area by climbing back up the A.T., north.

Trailhead Directions
The gravel Whitetop Mountain Road can be reached from Virginia 600. Drive 2.6 miles to the trail crossing from Virginia 600, north of US 58. Whitetop Mountain Road continues ahead to a public picnic grounds and then on to the summit of Whitetop Mountain.

STRAIGHT MOUNTAIN

MODERATE
2 miles roundtrip
1 hour

This day hike leads to the summit of Straight Mountain (elevation 3,500 feet), above the nearly 1,000-foot walls of Whitetop Laurel Gorge. The summit affords good southern views of Whitetop, Beach, Laurel and Chestnut Mountains.

The Hike
From US 58, follow the blue-blazed logging road .6 mile to its junction with the A.T. From here, begin your ascent of Straight Mountain along switchbacks. You can hear Whitetop Laurel Creek below you.

At mile 1.1, pass a cleared area that affords good views to the south of Whitetop Laurel Gorge (below) and Chestnut Mountain (above). Hike another .4 mile to the junction of an old logging road along a narrow ridge with a steep slope to the left. A short distance later, turn left off the road and begin to climb through the woods.

At mile 1.7, reach the junction with a blue-blazed trail that leads about .1 mile to the Saunders Shelter. Water is available from a spring a short distance past the shelter. Continue to climb the ridge for another .25 mile to the summit of Straight Mountain.

From here, return to the parking area by following the A.T. north to the blue-blazed logging road and following the road to US 58.

Trailhead Directions
The blue-blazed logging road is on US 58 just south of the Beartree Day Use Area access road.

TENNESSEE

NORTH CAROLINA

TENNESSEE/NORTH CAROLINA

Because so many miles of the Appalachian Trail traverse the Tennessee/North Carolina border, these two states are usually placed together in trail guides. Combined, the two states offer more than 370 miles of trail. Heading south, the trail begins in Tennessee (heading north, in North Carolina).

For the first 37 miles, the trail traverses the ridgeline as it makes its way to Wautaga Lake near Hampton, Tennessee. From Hampton, the trail heads through Laurel Fork Gorge with its spectacular waterfalls, and continues up White Rocks Mountain before it descends to Elk Park, North Carolina.

From Elk Park, a strenuous climb up to the Hump Mountains brings you to Grassy Ridge (a 6,000-foot grassy bald), Roan Highlands, Roan High Knob and Roan High Bluff. Roan High Bluff, over 6,000 feet in elevation, is known for its spectacular rhododendron gardens that bloom profusely each June. From Roan, the trail continues along the Tennessee/North Carolina border for nearly 100 miles as it makes its way to Hot Springs, North Carolina, and heads into the Great Smoky Mountains National Park. In this section, the trail passes Little Rock Knob, Unaka Mountain and Beauty Spot. It descends to Erwin, Tennessee, and continues to Hot Springs.

From Hot Springs, it is just over 30 miles to Davenport Gap, the northern entrance of the A.T. into the Smoky Mountains. In the Smokies, the trail traverses Mount Cammerer, the Sawteeth, and Charlies Bunion, reaches Newfound Gap, and proceeds to Clingmans Dome, the highest point on the entire A.T. (elevation 6,643 feet).

The A.T. continues across Silers Bald to Thunderhead and Rocky Top and down to the grassy area of Spence and Russell Fields. It then continues along to Shuckstack, and descends to Fontana Dam at the Little Tennessee

River, the southern boundary of the Great Smoky Mountains National Park.

From the Smokies, the A.T. ascends into the Nantahalas, where there are 4,000 and 5,000 foot peaks. The area between Fontana and Wesser is said to be one of the toughest sections on the A.T. From the Nantahala Outdoor Center at Wesser, the A.T. climbs up to Wesser Bald, Wayah Bald and Silers Bald before heading up the ridge to Standing Indian Mountain. Albert Mountain is also a notable climb in this section. From Albert, it is not far to the North Carolina/Georgia border at Bly Gap.

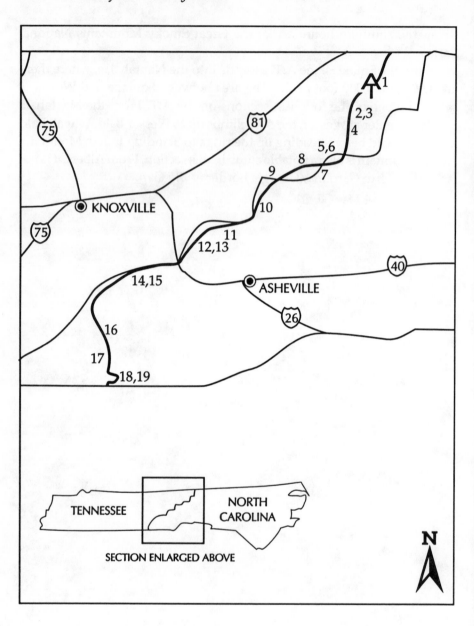

TENNESSEE

NORTH CAROLINA

SECTION ENLARGED ABOVE

N

1. Iron Mountain
2. Laurel Fork Gorge and Falls
3. Laurel Fork Gorge and Falls II
4. White Rocks Mountain Loop
5. Grassy Ridge
6. Roan Mountain
7. Little Rock Knob
8. Cliff Ridge
9. Big Bald
10. White Rocks Cliffs and Blackstack Cliffs
11. Lovers Leap Rock
12. Max Patch
13. Max Patch-Lemon Gap Traverse
14. Charlies Bunion
15. Clingmans Dome and Mount Collins
16. Wesser Bald
17. Siler Bald
18. Standing Indian Mountain
19. Ravenrock Ridge

Iron Mountain

MODERATE
8.8 miles roundtrip
4 1/2 hours

This hike will take you from the shore of Watauga Lake to two viewpoints high above the lake at rock outcrops on Iron Mountain. The entire hike is in the Big Laurel Branch Wilderness Area.

The Hike
From Watauga Dam Road, hike north on the A.T. and begin climbing Iron Mountain. As you climb along the ridge, the trail skirts highpoints, keeping a moderate grade. At mile 2.8, reach the junction with the blue-blazed Iron Mountain Trail to the left. Continue following the A.T., and at mile 1.2, reach a rock outcrop on the left with superior views of Watauga Lake. Hike another .4 mile to Vandeventer Shelter. The rock outcrop behind the shelter offers a fine view of the lake about 600 feet below.

To return, hike south on the A.T. to the trailhead on Watauga Dam Road.

Trailhead Directions
To reach the trailhead, take Tennessee 91 to the community of Hunter, turn left through the community of Siam, and continue to Watauga Dam Road. The trailhead is 9 miles east of Elizabethton, Tennessee.

Laurel Fork Gorge and Falls

EASY
5 miles roundtrip
2 1/2 hours

This leisurely hike will take you into the heart of rugged Laurel Fork Gorge. The vertical walls of the gorge rise more than 100 feet above the stream in some places. Pond and Black Mountains also tower over the gorge, rising well over 1,000 feet above Laurel Fork. The destination of this hike is the forty-foot tall Laurel Falls. There are many wildflowers and flowering shrubs that bloom, in season, in the gorge. The most well known include the Catawba and Carolina rhododendrons and mountain laurel, which usually bloom by late May. Because the A.T. is the only trail to these popular falls, the area can be quite crowded on spring and summer weekends.

The Hike
From the trailhead, follow the blue-blazed trail into the Gorge. At mile .4, pass "Buckled Rock," a rock wall across the stream from the trail. Hike another .6 mile to the junction with the A.T. Follow the A.T. south, hiking upstream along Laurel Fork for .25 mile, and cross the stream on a footbridge. The trail beyond the bridge climbs and briefly follows a ridge where there are good views of the gorge. Reach the junction with the side trail to Laurel Fork Shelter. The trail then drops down off the low ridge and at mile 2.3, skirts the base of a cliff on a built-up section of trail. Hike another .25 to the base of Laurel Falls.

To return, hike north on the A.T. to the blue-blazed trail leading back to the trailhead.

Trailhead Directions
The blue-blazed trail into the gorge is on the east side of Hampton, Tennessee, where US 321 crosses Laurel Fork on a bridge. There have been numerous reports of vandalism to cars left overnight in this area.

LAUREL FORK GORGE AND FALLS II

EASY
2.6 miles roundtrip
1 1/2 hours

This leisurely hike will take you into the heart of rugged Laurel Fork Gorge. The vertical walls of the gorge rise more than 100 feet above the stream in some places. Pond and Black Mountains also tower over the gorge, rising well over 1,000 feet above Laurel Fork. The destination of this hike is the forty-foot tall Laurel Falls. There are many wildflowers and flowering shrubs that bloom, in season, in the gorge. The most well known include the Catawba and Carolina rhododendrons and mountain laurel, which usually bloom by late May. Because the A.T. is the only trail to these popular falls, the area can be quite crowded on spring and summer weekends.

The Hike
From the USFS parking area in Dennis Cove, hike south on the A.T. The first .75 mile of this hike follows an old railroad grade to a bridge crossing over the stream. This bridge was built using wood from this wilderness area and without the benefit of power tools. It is a testament to the dedication and ingenuity of trail builders and maintainers. The trail continues to follow the old railroad bed, and at mile .9, reaches the junction with the blue-blazed trail to Potato Top. The .25 mile side trail leads to a spectacular view of Laurel Fork Gorge. Hike another .2 mile to where the trail leaves the railroad bed and descends steeply into the gorge. Laurel Falls is reached at mile 1.3.

The return hike is north on the A.T. to the parking area at Dennis Cove.

Trailhead Directions
The trailhead is at a USFS parking area on Dennis Cove Road. From US 321 in Hampton, Tennessee, drive to the town of Braemer, .5 mile east on Tennessee 67. Turn right in Braemer on USFS 50 (Dennis Cove Road). The parking area is on the left in 3 miles.

WHITE ROCKS MOUNTAIN LOOP

STRENUOUS
10 mile loop
6 hours

The terrain on this day hike (which includes a 1,000-foot elevation gain in 2.8 miles) is widely varied. The trail from Dennis Cove to the crest of White Rocks Mountain passes through open fields and by several interesting viewpoints and rock formations. The forest here is especially pretty.

The White Rocks Mountain Firetower offers panoramic views of Holston Mountain Range and Iron Mountain Range to the north, Beech Mountain and Grandfather Mountain to the east, the Roan Mountain area to the south, and Unaka Mountain to the southwest.

The Hike

From the parking area at USFS 50 at Dennis Cove, cross the road and head south along the A.T. Hike up through the woods for .1 mile to a shed near a chalet, leave the woods, and head up a road to the left of a pond.

At mile .25, head left, cross a fence to the right into a white pine forest, and parallel the fence for a short distance. Turn right, cross a short ridge into another drainage, turn left, and climb along a stream, crossing the stream several times in the next .6 mile.

At the head of a hollow (mile .9), head left and continue along a sidehill trail for .1 mile. Hike another .25 mile or so to a cliff at the end of a spur that affords good views both to the north and west. Turn right, and climb the ridge, heading through rhododendron.

At mile 1.5, reach another cliff on the right that offers good views to the west and north. Hike .25 mile, and turn right where the former A.T. (blue blazes) joins the trail from the left. From here, hike another 1.1 miles to White Rocks Mountain Firetower at the summit of White Rocks Mountain (elevation 4,105 feet).

Continue along the A.T., descending along a USFS road to where the road drops off the crest of the ridge at mile 3.3. Continue on the A.T., climbing for .25 to the edge of a field. The trail to the right descends several miles to US 19E. The A.T. continues southeast across the field, passing the former site of the old Canute Place, named for those who settled the area. Foundation stones, covered by a briar patch, are all that remain of the homestead.

Hike .1 mile to the junction with a blue-blazed trail that leads a short distance to a spring, and shortly thereafter, reach the remains of an old fence, enter the woods, and begin to climb to the left of the old fence.

At mile 4.4, reach the fence corner, and hike .5 mile along level trail to the highest point of White Rocks Mountain (elevation 4,206 feet). From here, return to the firetower via the A.T. north and hike 1.1 miles to the blue-blazed route of the former A.T. Follow the blue blazes .75 mile to Coon Den Falls and another .5 mile to USFS 50 at Dennis Cove. Follow USFS 50 .6 mile to the left to reach the parking area.

Trailhead Directions

The trailhead is at a USFS parking area on Dennis Cove Road. From US 321 in Hampton, Tennessee, drive to the town of Braemer, .5 mile east on Tennessee 67. Turn right in Braemer on USFS 50 (Dennis Cove Road). The parking area is on the left in 3 miles.

GRASSY RIDGE

MODERATE
4.2 miles roundtrip
2 1/2 hours

The destination of this day hike is Grassy Ridge, a southern Appalachian bald that is both over 6,000 feet in elevation and offers a 360-degree view. All other peaks of this elevation near the A.T. are either covered with trees or are topped with man-made structures (such as Clingmans Dome).

From Grassy Ridge, there are views of Grandfather Mountain, Beech Mountain and White Rocks Mountain. Rhododendron, flame azalea and Gray's lily can all be found blooming in this area in late June.

The Hike

From the parking area at Carvers Gap (elevation 5,512 feet), head north on the A.T. Climb stone steps, cross a rail fence on a stile, and then climb up the open slope of Round Bald. You will climb along a gravel trail with log steps, and as you near the summit, you will pass a stand of spruce. These were planted a long time ago to see if spruce would grow on a bald.

At mile .4, pass to the left of Round Bald summit (elevation 5,826 feet) and begin to descend along an old road. Hike another .25 mile, turn right onto a graded trail, and pass from the Tennessee to the North Carolina side of the ridge. Hike another .25 mile to Engine Gap, named for an abandoned sawmill engine. From here, begin to climb, passing a rock formation where there are good views at mile 1.

Reach the summit of Jane Bald (elevation 5,807 feet) in .1 mile, and begin to descend for .5 mile until the trail narrows and leaves the main crest of the ridge. Head left onto a trail that passes through alderbrush. The wide trail straight ahead of you leads to the flat summit of Grassy Bald.

If you take this wide trail, turn right near the summit through an open field scattered with alder brush, and reach a gap (elevation 6,050 feet) that is surrounded by Catawba rhododendron. This gap is .25 mile from the summit. There is a spring a short distance down the eastern side of the gap, and a rock outcropping with excellent views is .25 mile south of the gap.

To continue along the A.T., follow the narrower trail for .1 mile to a spring on your right. Continue to skirt the northern slope of Grassy Ridge for .4 mile to the eastern shoulder of Grassy Ridge. Do not turn left and descend. Instead, return to the parking area at Carvers Gap by following the A.T. south.

Trailhead Directions
The parking area at Carvers Gap is on the Tennessee/North Carolina state line, 14 miles south of Roan Mountain, Tennessee, on Tennessee 143 or 14 miles north of Bakersville, North Carolina, on North Carolina 261.

ROAN MOUNTAIN

MODERATE
3.8 miles roundtrip
2 hours

Roan Mountain and its spruce and fir covered summit is the destination of this day hike. Roan High Bluff, a summit of Roan Mountain, has an elevation of 6,267 feet, Roan High Knob, an elevation of 6,285 feet. In late June, when the rhododendron are blooming, nearby Cloudland Rhododendron Garden is definitely worth the short side trip. Here you will find Catawba rhododendron growing in such profusion that it seems as if surely they must have been planted on purpose. But, many balds in the southern Appalachians—Craggy Gardens on the Blue Ridge Parkway and Grayson Highlands near Mount Rogers in Virginia—boast magnificent concentrations of rhododendron growth.

The Hike
From the parking area at Carvers Gap (elevation 5,512 feet), follow the A.T. south along the log fence that follows the paved Cloudland Rhododendron Garden Road. There is water here at a spring below the picnic area to right.

You will soon leave the road and climb along a trail through weeds and balsam. At mile .25, reach an old road, turn right, and follow the road through balsam and rhododendron nearly all the way to Cloudland. Climb along switchbacks and reach the junction with a blue-blazed trail at mile 1.3. The trail heads left .1 mile to the summit of Roan High Knob where a shelter (an old fire warden's cabin) is located. This is the highest shelter on the entire A.T. A spring is located a short distance behind the cabin.

The A.T. continues along the road and reaches an open picnic area in another .5 mile. The trail continues past the picnic area, and a short distance later, passes through rhododendron. At the fork, turn left and climb, crossing an old trail.

At mile 1.9, reach an old cabin site, turn left, and shortly thereafter, enter the woods and continue to climb. You will soon leave the woods and climb through a grassy area with large spruce trees. Here, you are at the left front corner of the site of the old Cloudland Hotel (elevation 6,150 feet). Ahead and to your right is a small parking lot. To the left, beyond the lot, is a larger lot built in 1952. The road beyond the parking lot leads to the rhododendron gardens. Water can be obtained at drinking fountains here. Just beyond this area is Roan High Bluff.

Return to the parking area at Carvers Gap by following the A.T. north.

Trailhead Directions

The parking area at Carvers Gap is on the Tennessee/North Carolina state line, 14 miles south of Roan Mountain, Tennessee, on Tennessee 143 or 14 miles north of Bakersville, North Carolina, on North Carolina 261.

LITTLE ROCK KNOB

STRENUOUS
2.6 miles roundtrip
2 1/2 hours

This is a tough little hike. The elevation changes 1,000 feet in the 1.3 miles from Hughes Gap to Little Rock Knob. However, the knob will richly reward you for your efforts, offering a magnificent view of the valley below. This hike is not as popular as the nearby Roan Mountain, and it is a better choice for weekend hikers looking for a nice hike without the crowds attracted to Roan on pretty spring and summer days.

The Hike

The hike starts on the same side of the gap as the small dirt parking area. Follow the A.T. south as it gradually ascends up to a highpoint on the ridge in .25 mile. At mile .4, cross a second highpoint on the ridge and descend to a gap. The trail climbs sharply from the gap and never reaches the summit of the knob. At mile 1.3, reach a rock outcrop on Little Rock Knob. There are excellent views from this lookout. Look north to view White Rocks Mountain, which the A.T. passes over.

To return, hike north on the A.T. to the trailhead at Hughes Gap.

Trailhead Directions

From the town of Roan Mountain, Tennessee, take Tennessee 143, 5.25

miles to the community of Burbank. Hughes Gap Road forks to the right off of Tennessee 143 in Burbank. The trail is 3 miles farther on Hughes Gap Road. Parking is on the right side of the road in a small dirt parking area.

From the North Carolina side, Hughes Gap Road turns off of North Carolina 226 in the small town of Buladean, North Carolina. From Buladean, it is 4 miles to the trailhead on the left.

CLIFF RIDGE

MODERATE
3 miles roundtrip
2 hours

This hike takes you from the banks of the Nolichucky to a cliff above the river, which provides many fine viewpoints. The trail follows Cliff Ridge for a mile. The walkway on the bridge over the Nolichucky River is named the Ray Hunt Walkway in honor of a longtime trail maintainer, who served as Chair of the Appalachian Trail Conference from 1983-1989.

The Hike
From the trailhead at the bridge, follow the road to the left and shortly thereafter, climb up the bank on steps. In .25 mile, the trail begins to ascend on switchbacks. At mile .5, reach the southern end of Cliff Ridge. For the next 1 mile, the trail continues to climb as it parallels the cliff. To the left, there are many fine views through the trees and from rock outcroppings.

To return, hike north on the A.T. to the trailhead.

Trailhead Directions
The trailhead at the Nolichucky River is in Chestoa, Tennessee, on Tennessee 36, .5 mile east of US 23 and just over 2 miles south of Erwin, Tennessee.

BIG BALD

MODERATE
7.8 miles roundtrip
4 1/2 hours

Big Bald is perhaps the finest example of a southern Appalachian bald mountain. From its treeless summit, the bald offers an outstanding 360-degree view. You can see several mountain ranges including the Blacks, Great Smokies, Nantahalas and Unaka Mountains.

There are many theories about how the balds were created. Some have attributed balds to fires caused by lightning, Indians burning the trees off to clear the mountains, settlers clearing pasture land, or even UFOs. Whatever the original cause, most balds have been kept clear at one point through grazing. Without being grazed or cut with mowers, the balds would become covered with trees in time, as plant succession does its work.

The Hike

From the dirt road in Street Gap, hike north on the A.T. Follow the dirt road leading through the fence, and follow it up the ridge for .6 mile to where the dirt road continues straight ahead and the trail turns to the right. Hike another .4 mile and reach the junction with a short blue-blazed trail leading to a spring on left.

At mile 3.1, reach the junction with a second short blue-blazed trail leading to a spring on left, and at mile 3.2, reach the junction with another blue-blazed trail on right. Hike .3 mile to an open meadow, and continue to climb on Big Bald. The trail is cut into the sod through the meadow and is easy to follow as it ascends to the summit of Big Bald (elevation 5,516 feet) at mile 3.9. On a clear day, there is an unsurpassed view of many of the mountains that western North Carolina is known for.

To return, hike south on the A.T. to Street Gap.

Trailhead Directions

The road up to Street Gap is unimproved and can be difficult for some cars. From US 23 in Sams Gap on the Tennessee/North Carolina state line, it is 6 miles to the road up to Street Gap. It is about 3 miles up to the trailhead on that road. Do not take any of the three roads that turn off to the left during the climb up the mountain.

WHITE ROCKS CLIFFS
AND BLACKSTACK CLIFFS

EASY
4.4 miles roundtrip
2 hours

This hike offers spectacular views from two rocky ridges. The highest point east of the Mississippi, Mount Mitchell (elevation 6,684 feet), and the rest of the Black Mountains can be seen from this hike. There is little change in elevation on the hike because the drive to the trailhead brings you to the top of the ridge.

The Hike
From the trailhead at the Camp Creek Bald Firetower, hike .25 mile to the junction with the A.T. Turn left on the A.T. and hike north, descending .75 mile to an old logging road. At mile 1.9, climb via switchbacks, and in another .1 mile, reach the junction with the short side trail leading to White Rocks Cliffs. After enjoying the view at White Rocks, return to the trail and continue hiking north. Hike another .25 mile to the junction with a short side trail leading to Blackstack Cliffs.

To return, hike south on the A.T. to the .25-mile side trail leading up to Camp Creek Bald Firetower.

Trailhead Directions
From Tennessee 70, .5 mile north of the North Carolina state line at Allen Gap, the USFS fire road follows Paint Creek up to its headwaters and continues on to the firetower on the summit of Camp Creek Bald (elevation 4,844 feet). There are fine views from the firetower, but they lack the drama that the cliffs add to the views.

LOVERS LEAP ROCK

STRENUOUS
2.6 miles roundtrip
2 hours

This short, sometimes steep hike leads to Lovers Leap, which provides outstanding views of the French Broad River and the town of Hot Springs, North Carolina. There is a 500 foot drop from Lovers Leap to the river below. The rock's name is said to date back to an Indian maiden who threw herself from the cliff after learning her lover had been killed by a jealous beau.

The hike begins in the town of Hot Springs, where the A.T. passes through town on a sidewalk alongside the main street. There is a 1,000 foot change in elevation from the town to the overlook, making this a difficult, though short hike.

The Hike

From the USFS district office in Hot Springs, hike north on the A.T. and follow the white blazes down the sidewalk. Cross Spring Creek on a small bridge, and at mile .25, cross the French Broad River on a bridge. Turn right as the trail follows Silvermine Creek Road. Follow the trail as it parallels the river, passing by the Nantahala Outdoor Center. At mile .9, begin climbing up to Lovers Leap on switchbacks. Reach an overlook with outstanding views in .25 mile and then continue another .25 mile to Lovers Leap Rock at the junction of the Silver Mine Trail.

To return, hike south on the A.T. to the USFS office in Hot Springs.

Trailhead Directions

The trailhead is at the USFS district ranger's office on US 25/70 in Hot Springs, North Carolina. Hot Springs is 17 miles east of Newport, Tennessee, and 40 miles northwest of Asheville, North Carolina. Inquire at the office before leaving your car. Parking is also available along the main road in town.

Max Patch

MODERATE
1.6 miles roundtrip
1 1/2 hours

The trail gently climbs up the side of the mountain to the treeless summit of Max Patch. There is an outstanding panoramic view of the Blacks, Balds, Balsams and Great Smoky Mountains from this southernmost bald mountain on the A.T. On a clear day, you can see the highest point in the eastern United States, Mount Mitchell (elevation 6,684 feet), to the east. In the spring, there are many wildflowers in bloom along this section of trail.

The Hike
From the trailhead, hike north on the A.T. and pass through a stile. Enter the woods and descend .1 mile to a small creek. Begin to ascend, slowly at first, and cross a gravel road in .25 mile. The trail climbs Max Patch on log steps cut into the hillside and then crosses the grass to the broad summit of the mountain (elevation 4,629 feet).

To return, hike south on the A.T. to the trailhead on Max Patch Road.

Trailhead Directions
Turn onto North Carolina 1175 from North Carolina 209 at a point approximately 20 miles north of Interstate 40 near Lake Junaluska, North Carolina, and 7 miles south of Hot Springs, North Carolina. Follow North Carolina 1175 for 5.3 miles, and then turn onto Max Patch Road (North Carolina 1182). The parking area at the foot of the bald is 3 miles down Max Patch Road.

Max Patch-Lemon Gap Traverse

MODERATE
6.2 mile traverse
4 hours

The trail gently climbs up the side of the mountain to the treeless summit of Max Patch. There is an outstanding panoramic view of the Blacks, Balds, Balsams and Great Smoky Mountains from this southernmost bald mountain on the A.T. On a clear day, you can see the highest point in the eastern

United States, Mount Mitchell (elevation 6,684 feet), to the east. In the spring, there are many wildflowers in bloom along this section of trail.

The hike continues from Max Patch, descending and passing several good views of the cascades on Roaring Fork. The trail to Lemon Gap offers a variety of scenery, everything from rhododendron and hemlocks to hardwoods.

Because this day hike is a traverse, it will require a shuttle or two vehicles.

The Hike

From the trailhead, hike north on the A.T. and pass through a stile. Enter the woods and descend .1 mile to a small creek. Begin to ascend, slowly at first, crossing a gravel road in .25 mile. The trail climbs Max Patch on log steps cut into the hillside and then crosses the grass to the broad summit of the mountain (elevation 4,629 feet).

Hike another .25 mile to the junction of a trail that leads left to North Carolina 1182. At mile 1.2, cross a stile, enter the woods, and descend .25 mile to two more stiles. Between the stiles, the A.T. passes a piped spring. At mile 1.6, begin climbing to a meadow on Buckeye Ridge, and reach another stile at mile 2.

Soon thereafter, cross a road and descend through rhododendron and hemlock to steps. Descend steps to a stream crossing, and at mile 2.4, descend steps and a ramp to an old railroad bed. In .4 mile, cross stream again and reach the junction with a road that heads left to North Carolina 1182. Turn right, ascend, cross several footbridges, and then descend to bridge crossing at mile 3.7.

Reach the junction of a road that leads left to North Carolina 1182, climb the ramp into open woods, and cross the stream three times. At mile 4.5, cross old woods road, and at mile 4.8, cross severeal footbridges in the next .25 mile. Reach the junction with the side trail to Roaring Fork Shelter at mile 5.8, and in the next .25 mile, cross a log bridge and a stream.

Reach Lemon Gap (elevation 3,550 feet) at mile 6.2. North Carolina 1182 is to your left. The road heads north into Tennessee as Tennessee 107 and south into North Carolina as North Carolina 1182.

Trailhead Directions

Turn onto North Carolina 1175 from North Carolina 209 at a point approximately 20 miles north of Interstate 40 near Lake Junaluska, North Carolina, and 7 miles south of Hot Springs, North Carolina. Follow North

Carolina 1175 for 5.3 miles, and then turn onto Max Patch Road (North Carolina 1182). The parking area at the foot of the bald is 3 miles down Max Patch Road. The trailhead at Lemon Gap is farther down the road where North Carolina 1182 becomes Tennessee 107.

CHARLIES BUNION

GREAT SMOKY MOUNTAINS NATIONAL PARK

STRENUOUS
7.8 miles roundtrip
5 hours

Charlies Bunion, an exposed, rocky knob is the destination of this day hike. From this knob, there are several outstanding views—Jump-off and Mount Kephart to the west, Mount LeConte to the northwest, the gorges of the headwaters of Porters Creek to the north, Greenbriar Pinnacle to the northeast, and the Sawteeth Range to the east. Take care when climbing around the Bunion; a man fell to his death here in 1990.

The Hike

From the parking area at Newfound Gap (elevation 5,045 feet), follow the A.T. from the northeast corner of the parking area east along a graded trail. Red spruce and Fraser fir (also called balsams) are common in this section. At mile 1.7, reach the junction with the Sweat Heifer Creek Trail, probably named for the cattle drives up this steep trail to the grassy balds where the livestock was grazed. The Sweat Heifer Creek Trail heads down to Kephart Prong.

In another .25 mile, you will have good views to the southwest of Clingmans Dome (elevation 6,643 feet), the highest point on the A.T. Thomas Ridge and Oconaluftee River Gorge are to the south. At mile 2.4, hike along the North Carolina/Tennessee state line, and descend from a 6,000-foot elevation to the junction with the Boulevard Trail in another .25 mile.

The Boulevard Trail heads 5.3 miles to LeConte Lodge and Shelter. You will take the right fork at this junction and skirt the North Carolina side of Mount Kephart. At mile 3, reach the site of Icewater Spring Shelter, which was closed in 1994 due to overuse. The site of the first privy in the Smokies, sanitation problems were the predominant reason for the shelter's closure. There is a good spring a short distance further along the A.T.

In another .6 mile, pass through a .75 mile section with outstanding views because of a fire that occurred after timbering operations in 1925. It is only .25 mile from the beginning of this section to the western peak of Charlies Bunion. You will skirt the left side of this peak, arriving at the higher peak in .1 mile. The lower, western peak is sometimes called Fodder Stack, for its similarity in shape to a stack of hay (or fodder).

To return to Newfound Gap, hike south on the A.T.

Trailhead Directions
The parking area at Newfound Gap can be reached by taking US 441 16 miles from Gatlinburg, Tennessee, or 20 miles from Cherokee, North Carolina.

CLINGMANS DOME AND MOUNT COLLINS

GREAT SMOKY MOUNTAINS NATIONAL PARK

MODERATE
6.8 miles roundtrip
3 hours

This day hike will take you to the highest point on the A.T.—Clingmans Dome (elevation 6,643 feet). On clear days, there are outstanding views of the peaks of the Great Smokies from the observation tower. Formerly Smoky Dome, the peak is named after Thomas L. Clingman, a Civil War General and U.S. Senator. Clingman is known for his heated debate with Elisha Mitchell. The two argued over which peak in the state was the highest—Grandfather Mountain or Balsam Mountain. The debate took place through editorials in rival Asheville, North Carolina, newspapers. Mitchell died in a fall while trying to prove his claim that Balsam Mountain was the tallest. History proved Mitchell right, however, and the highest peak east of the Mississippi bears his name.

Clingmans Dome features an observation tower with signs identifying the distant mountains. The section of the A.T. from Clingmans Dome north to Newfound Gap was constructed by the CCC between 1939 and 1940; this hike will take you along the ridge from Clingmans Dome through a spruce and balsam forest and over the summits of Mount Love and Mount Collins.

The Hike

From the parking area at Clingmans Dome, hike .5 mile along a paved path to the observation tower. It is a short walk along a side trail (rare mountain cranberry abounds here) to the A.T. From Clingmans Dome, you will descend into a gap before climbing to the summit of Mount Love (elevation 6,446 feet). Descend moderately to Collins Gap (elevation 5,886 feet) at mile 2.8, then climb steeply to the summit of Mount Collins, which offers good views as you climb.

A short distance before reaching the summit of Mount Collins (elevation 6,188 feet), you will have good views over North Carolina. Once you reach the summit, you are at the end of this day hike.

Return to the Clingmans Dome parking area by retracing your steps back along the A.T. and taking the side trail to the observation tower and paved trail.

Trailhead Directions

The Clingmans Dome Road (closed in the winter) is accessible from Newfound Gap on US 441, 20 miles west of Cherokee, North Carolina, and 16 miles east of Gatlinburg, Tennessee. Clingmans Dome is 7.6 miles from Newfound Gap on Clingmans Dome Road.

WESSER BALD

STRENUOUS
2.8 miles roundtrip
2 hours

The spectacular views from Wesser Bald (elevation 4,627 feet) are the highlight of this day hike. An observation deck was recently completed on the steel frame of the Wesser Bald Firetower. The old tower was burned by vandals in 1979. The new observation tower was funded by the Appalachian Trail Conference, North Carolina's Trail Grant Program, and the Nantahala Hiking Club (with matching funds from the USFS Challenge Cost-share Program).

The Hike

From the parking area at Tellico Gap (elevation 3,850 feet), take the A.T. north. Head left along a graded trail that parallels the gravel road that leads to the firetower. From here, you will begin to climb Wesser Bald.

Climb 1.4 miles to the top of the rocky ledge and reach the junction with a side trail that heads right a short distance to the firetower and new observation deck, which offers great views of the surrounding mountain ranges.

To return, head south on the A.T. to Tellico Gap.

Trailhead Directions
The A.T. crossing at Tellico Gap can be reached via a 4-mile gravel road (North Carolina 1365) off of North Carolina 1310, which connects US 19 and US 64.

SILER BALD

STRENUOUS
3.8 miles roundtrip
2 1/2 hours

Siler Bald (elevation 5,216 feet) is the destination of this day hike. The bald was named for William Siler whose great-grandson, the Reverend Rufus A. Morgan, helped establish the A.T. in North Carolina. The USFS maintains the bald by keeping it cleared. From atop the bald, there are views back to Tray Mountain in Georgia and ahead to the Great Smokies.

The Hike
From the parking area just off North Carolina 1310 at Wayah Crest (elevation 4,180 feet), pass through the picnic area, pick up the trail, cross a dirt road, and climb up the bald along a graded footpath. At mile 1.7, reach a clearing used for grazing by deer and other wildlife. Look to your right to view the open summit of Siler Bald. The outstanding view from the summit can be reach via a .25-mile side trail.

To return to the parking area at Wayah Crest, follow the A.T. north.

Trailhead Directions
North Carolina 1310 can be reached from Franklin, North Carolina. There is a sign noting Wayah Crest and the picnic area.

STANDING INDIAN MOUNTAIN

STRENUOUS
5 miles roundtrip
3 hours

Standing Indian Mountain (elevation 5,498 feet) is the highest point on the A.T. south of the Smoky Mountains. A .1-mile side trip leads to the summit and spectacular views, both north and south, of the mountain ranges the A.T. follows.

The Hike
From the parking area at Deep Gap (elevation 4,341 feet), follow the A.T. north along a graded trail that parallels two logging roads. In .75 mile, cross a small stream; until 1995 this was the site of Standing Indian Shelter. The new shelter is on a short sidetrail. Continue to climb Standing Indian along a grassy road and reach an unmarked trail to the left that leads to a spring at mile 2.4. Shortly thereafter, reach the junction of the blue-blazed Lower Ridge Trail, which heads 4.2 miles left to Standing Indian Campground. Follow this trail to the right .1 mile to the summit of Standing Indian.

To return to the parking area at Deep Gap, follow the A.T. south.

Trailhead Directions
The parking area at Deep Gap can be reached by taking USFS 71 off of US 64 near the Clay-Macon County line. The road is marked and it is 6 miles from US 64 along USFS 71 to Deep Gap.

RAVENROCK RIDGE

STRENUOUS
9 miles roundtrip
5 hours

The cliffs at Ravenrock Ridge offer outstanding views of the Southern Nantahalas. Following the crest of the Blue Ridge, this hike offers views to the west of Shooting Creek Valley and Lake Chatuge on the Georgia/North Carolina border. You will also pass through parts of the Southern Nantahala Wilderness on this hike.

The Hike

From the parking area at Deep Gap, follow the A.T. south by heading right into the woods and climbing Yellow Mountain. In .75 mile, the trail switchbacks up to a rock outcropping and continues on to the highest point of this section, providing a view to the north. Hike 1 mile to Wateroak Gap in a small clearing. The A.T. continues up the ridge for another .9 mile to the junction with the blue-blazed Chunky Gal Trail, which heads 5.5 miles to US 64. Head left on the A.T. for .25 mile to the edge of a large, grassy area at Whiteoak Stamp. An overgrown trail to the left leads to an intermittent water source.

Follow the A.T. for another .75 mile to Muskrat Creek Shelter, just to the left of the trail. Continue on the A.T., cross a small stream, and reach the junction with a blue-blazed side trail that heads right about .5 mile to Ravenrock Ridge. Follow the side trail to Ravenrock Ridge.

To return to the parking area at Deep Gap, take the side trail back to the A.T., and the A.T. north to Deep Gap.

Trailhead Directions

The parking area at Deep Gap can be reached by taking USFS 71 off of US 64 near the Clay-Macon County line. The road is marked and it is 6 miles from US 64 along USFS 71 to Deep Gap.

GEORGIA

GEORGIA

Georgia is the last state on the trail (or the first for most thru-hikers). Its more than 75 miles are extremely popular year round. The trail traverses the Chattahoochee National Forest and is noted for its rugged wilderness areas and high elevations. Popular hiking spots include The Swag of the Blue Ridge, Tray Mountain, Rocky Mountain, Blue Mountain, Wolf Laurel Top, Blood Mountain and Big Cedar Mountain.

Neels Gap, at the base of Blood Mountain, offers the Walasi-Yi Mountain Crossings Center. It is the only building through which the A.T. passes. Springer Mountain is the southern terminus of the A.T. and features a recently rerouted trail and a new bronze plaque atop the summit.

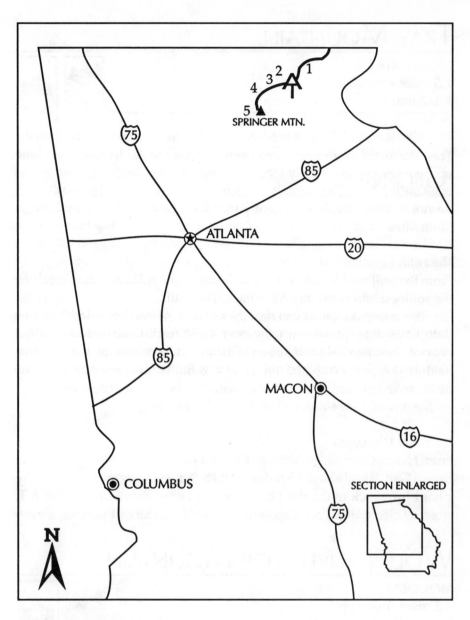

1. Tray Mountain
2. Wolf Laurel Top Mountain
3. Blood Mountain
4. Big Cedar Mountain
5. Springer Mountain

TRAY MOUNTAIN

MODERATE
1.6 miles roundtrip
1 1/2 hours

This hike is part of the 10.8 mile section of the A.T. that passes through the Tray Mountain Wilderness Area from Tray Gap to Addis Gap. The climb up from the gap is a steady ascent on switchbacks that brings you to this outstanding peak. The summit is covered with low trees and shrubs, which do not obstruct the magnificent panoramic view of the north Georgia Mountains.

The Hike
From the trailhead in Tray Gap, hike north on the A.T. and begin climbing the southern slope of Tray Mountain. The trail ascends on switchbacks, climbing more sharply as you near the summit. At mile .75, reach the rocky summit of Tray Mountain (elevation 4,430 feet). Georgia's two tallest peaks, Brasstown Bald and Rabun Bald, are visible to the north. Brasstown Bald is the peak with the tower and buildings on the summit. The distinctive rock face of Yonah Mountain can be seen to the south.

To return, hike south on the A.T. to Tray Gap.

Trailhead Directions
From Helen, Georgia, go north on Georgia 75. After passing by the A.T. in Unicoi Gap, travel about 4.5 miles to USFS 698 on the right. You must take a hard turn back to the right to get on the Forest Service road. The A.T. crosses USFS 698 at Tray Gap, where there is a small dirt parking area.

WOLF LAUREL TOP MOUNTAIN

MODERATE
4.2 miles roundtrip
2 1/2 hours

This day hike features excellent views from the summits of Cowrock Mountain and Wolf Laurel Top. There is a spectacular view from an open rock face atop Wolf Laurel Top. This entire hike is in the Raven Cliffs Wilderness Area.

The Hike

From the trailhead in Tesnatee Gap, follow the A.T. south, and begin the steady, sometimes steep, ascent of Cowrock Mountain. At mile .9, reach the summit of Cowrock Mountain (elevation 3,842 feet). There are a couple of good viewpoints from the mountain. One is from the rocks just before the trail reaches the summit. The others is to the left of the trail just after the summit. The distinctive rock face of Yonah Mountain can be seen from this viewpoint.

Descend Cowrock Mountain to Baggs Creek Gap. The trail from the gap to Wolf Laurel Top climbs gradually over the next 1.25 miles. Reach Wolf Laurel Top (elevation 3,766 feet) at mile 2.1. The outstanding view from the rocks is just to the left of the trail.

To return, hike north on the A.T. to the trailhead in Tesnatee Gap.

Trailhead Directions

From Helen, Georgia, go north on Georgia 75 to Georgia 356. From Georgia 356, go to Georgia 348 and turn right. It is about 12 miles from the town of Helen to the trailhead in Tesnatee Gap.

BLOOD MOUNTAIN

STRENUOUS
4.8 miles roundtrip
3 1/2 hours

This hike is, without a doubt, the most hiked section of the A.T. in Georgia. On pretty spring and summer weekends, this section of trail is often crowded. The reason for the hike's popularity is two-fold: it is easy to get to, and the rocky summit of Blood Mountain offers a superb view of the north Georgia Mountains.

On the summit of Blood Mountain, there is a stone cabin built by the CCC in the 1930s. The two-room shelter, intended for overnight use by A.T. hikers, is listed in the National Register of Historic Places. The mountain's name is said to date back to a fierce fight between the Creek and Cherokee Indians.

Also of interest in the area is the Walasi-Yi Mountain Crossings Center in Neels Gap. There is a hiking store with a good selection of equipment and books on the outdoors and the region. The only covered section of the A.T. passes through a walkway at the center.

The Hike

From the trailhead at the Byron Reese Park, follow the blue-blazed trail 1 mile to the junction with the A.T. Turn right on the A.T. and hike south, climbing more steeply on switchbacks and gaining nearly 1,000 feet in elevation in just over 1 mile. At mile 2.4, pass through an open rock face that offers an excellent view. Reach the tree-covered summit of Blood Mountain (elevation 4,461 feet) in .1 mile. There are outstanding views from the rock outcroppings around the shelter.

To return, hike north on the A.T. to the blue-blazed side trail, then follow the side trail to the parking area.

Trailhead Directions

The parking area at Byron Reese Memorial Park is .5 mile north of Neels Gap on US 19/129. Neels Gap is 12 miles south of Blairsville, Georgia, and 18 miles north of Cleveland, Georgia.

BIG CEDAR MOUNTAIN

MODERATE
2 miles roundtrip
1 1/2 hours

While not as spectacular as the views from Blood Mountain, the views from the side of Big Cedar are quite nice. This section of trail is also less frequented than Blood Mountain.

The Hike

From the trailhead in Woody Gap (elevation 3,150 feet), hike north on the A.T. (across the road from the picnic tables) and enter the woods. During the spring, there are numerous flame azaleas in bloom along this section of trail. Climb gradually, then descend to Lunsford Gap at mile .75. From here, the climb becomes steep. Reach a rocky overlook on the right side of the trail, near the summit of Big Cedar Mountain (elevation 3,737 feet) at mile 1. The view to the south is outstanding from this open rock face.

To return, hike is south on the A.T. to Woody Gap.

Trailhead Directions

From Dahlonega, Georgia, drive about 9 miles north on US 19 to its junction with Georgia 60 in Stone Pile Gap. Go north about 5.5 miles on Georgia 60 to Woody Gap. There is parking and a picnic area at the trailhead.

SPRINGER MOUNTAIN

MODERATE
1.8 miles roundtrip
1 1/2 hours

This short hike leads to the southern terminus of the A.T. A bronze plaque set into a rock face lies just past the southernmost white blaze. There is a fine view to the west from this open rock ledge.

Prior to 1958, the southern terminus of the trail had been on Mount Ogelthorpe. Real estate development in the area lead the Georgia Appalachian Trail Club to move the terminus to this more remote mountain within the bounds of the Chatahoochee National Forest.

The Hike
From the trailhead on USFS 42, hike south on the A.T. and begin the steady, gradual climb up Springer on a sidehill trail. At mile .75, reach the junction with the .25-mile side trail leading to Springer Mountain Shelter. For those who wonder how the large beams of the timber frame shelter were hiked up the mountain, they weren't. The beams were assembled and the framework was helicoptered to the shelter's present site in 1992. Hike another .25 mile to the end of the trail. There is a trail register in a mailbox on a tree near the rock face.

To return, hike north on the A.T. to USFS 42.

Trailhead Directions
To get to this trail crossing, take USFS 42 from Georgia 60 just north of Woody Gap. From Dahlonega, Georgia, drive about 9 miles north on US 19 to its junction with Georgia 60 in Stone Pile Gap. Go north about 5.5 miles on Georgia 60 to Woody Gap. There is parking and a picnic area at the trailhead. Just north of Woody Gap, turn left on USFS 42, which is paved for the first several miles, and continue to the trail crossing. You will cross the A.T. in Gooch, Cooper, and Hightower Gaps before coming to the trailhead near Springer. This road is often open when USFS 28 and 77 are not.

APPENDIX

TRAIL MAINTENANCE CLUBS

The Appalachian Trail owes its existence to the hiking clubs, which are charged with its maintenance. These clubs are responsible not only for the maintenance of the footpath but also for relocating the trail, managing its surrounding lands, helping with land acquisition negotiations, compiling and updating guidebook and map information, working with trail communities on both problems and special events, and recruiting and training new maintainers.

Addresses appear for those with permanent offices or post office boxes. In other cases, please contact ATC headquarters for the address of the current club president or other appropriate officer (P.O. Box 807, Harpers Ferry, West Virginia 25425).

Maine Appalachian Trail Club, P.O. Box 283, Augusta, ME 04330.
MATC covers 264 miles from Katahdin to ME 26 (Grafton Notch, ME).

Appalachian Mountain Club, 5 Joy Street, Boston, MA 02108.
AMC covers 119 miles from Grafton Notch, ME to Kinsman Notch, NH.

Dartmouth Outing Club, P.O. Box 9, Hanover, NH 03755.
DOC covers 75 miles from Kinsman Notch, NH to VT 12.

Green Mountain Club, Rural Route 1, Box 650, Waterbury Center, VT 05677.
GMC covers 116 miles from VT 12 to the Massachusetts border.

AMC—Berkshire Chapter, 5 Joy Street, Boston, MA 02108.
The Berkshire Chapter covers 87 miles from the Vermont border to Sages Ravine, MA.

AMC—Connecticut Chapter, 5 Joy Street, Boston, MA 02108.
The Connecticut Chapter covers 50 miles from Sages Ravine, MA to the New York border.

The New York-New Jersey Trail Conference, 232 Madison Avenue, Room 908, New York, NY 10016.
NY-NJTC covers 163 miles from the Connecticut border to Delaware Water Gap, PA.

Keystone Trails Association, P.O. Box 251, Cogan Station, PA 17728.

KTA is the blanket association for the following 10 independent trail clubs, all of which can be contacted at the above address.

Springfield Trail Club: 7 miles from Delaware Water Gap, PA to Fox Gap, PA.

Batona Hiking Club: 8 miles from Fox Gap, PA to Wind Gap, PA.

AMC—Delaware Valley Chapter: 16 miles from Wind Gap, PA to Little Gap, PA.

Philadelphia Trail Club: 10 miles from Little Gap, PA to Lehigh Furnace Gap, PA.

Blue Mountain Eagle Climbing Club: Split into two sections—66 miles from Lehigh Furnace Gap, PA to Bake Oven Knob, PA and from Tri-County Corner, PA to Rausch Creek, PA.

Allentown Hiking Club: 12 miles from Bake Oven Knob, PA to Tri-County Corner, PA.

Brandywine Valley Outing Club: 11 miles from Rausch Creek, PA to PA 325.

Susquehanna Appalachian Trail Club: 9 miles from PA 325 to PA 225.

York Hiking Club: 8 miles from PA 225 to the Susquehanna River.

Cumberland Valley Appalachian Trail Management Association: 18 miles from Darlington Trail to Center Point Knob.

Mountain Club of Maryland: 30 miles from the Susquehanna River to Darlington Trail and from Center Point Knob to Pine Grove Furnace State Park, PA.

Potomac Appalachian Trail Club, 118 Park Street S.E., Vienna, VA 22180-4609.

The PATC covers 238 miles from Pine Grove Furnace State Park, PA, to Rockfish Gap, VA.

Old Dominion Appalachian Trail Club, P.O. Box 25283, Richmond, VA 23260-5283.

ODATC covers 17 miles from Rockfish Gap, VA to Reeds Gap, VA.

Tidewater Appalachian Trail Club, P.O. Box 8246, Norfolk, VA 23503.

Tidewater covers 10 miles from Reeds Gap, VA to Tye River, VA.

Natural Bridge Appalachian Trail Club, P.O. Box 3012, Lynchburg, VA 24503.

NBATC covers 88 miles from the Tye River, VA to Black Horse Gap, VA.

Roanoke Appalachian Trail Club. Contact ATC for current address.

RATC covers 114 miles from Black Horse Gap, VA to Stony Creek Valley, VA.

Kanawha Trail Club. Contact ATC for current address.

Kanawha covers 21 miles from Stony Creek Valley, VA to New River, VA.

Virginia Tech Outing Club. Contact ATC for current address.

Virginia Tech covers 25 miles from VA 608 to Garden Mountain, VA.

Piedmont Appalachian Trail Hikers, P.O. Box 4423, Greensboro, NC 27404.

PATH covers 43 miles from Garden Mountain, VA to VA 16.

Mount Rogers Appalachian Trail Club. Contact ATC for current address.

Mount Rogers covers 64 miles from VA 16 to Damascus, VA.

Tennessee Eastman Hiking Club, P.O. Box 511, Kingsport, TN 37662.

TEHC covers 126 miles from Damascus, VA, to Spivey Gap, NC.

Carolina Mountain Club. Contact ATC for current address.

CMC covers 90 miles from Spivey Gap, NC, to Davenport Gap, TN/NC.

The Smoky Mountains Hiking Club. Contact ATC for current address.

Smoky Mountains covers 97 miles from Davenport Gap, TN/NC, to the Nantahala River, NC.

Nantahala Hiking Club, 31 Carl Slagle Road, Franklin, NC 28734.

NHC covers 60 miles from the Nantahala River to Bly Gap on the Georgia border.

Georgia Appalachian Trail Club, P.O. Box 654, Atlanta, GA 30301.

GATC covers 78 miles from the North Carolina border to Springer Mountain.